essentials
of business
policy

DAVID C. D. ROGERS

Professor of Business Administration
The University of Michigan
Graduate School of Business Administration

essentials of business policy

HARPER & ROW, PUBLISHERS
New York
Evanston
San Francisco
London

Sponsoring Editor: John Greenman
Project Editor: Pamela Landau
Designer: Jared Pratt
Production Supervisor: Stefania J. Taflinska

**ESSENTIALS
OF BUSINESS
POLICY**

Library of Congress Cataloging in Publication Data

Rogers, David C D
  Essentials of business policy.

  Includes index.
  1. Industrial management. 2. Planning. I. Title.
HD31.R623   658.4'01   75-2326
ISBN 0-06-045544-6

To Edmund P. Learned

CONTENTS

PREFACE

This concise introduction to the complex and rapidly growing field of corporate strategy and long-range planning was compiled in response to the pleas of thousands of students—MBA's and practicing managers alike—over the past 17 years. In fact, portions of this book were written and distributed to students as far back as 1962 in order to provide a conceptual framework for case studies and individual experiences.

The subject matter is the allocation of scarce resources: human, financial, physical assets, or intangibles. Conceptually speaking, *strategy* is the *direction* of such resource allocation, while *planning* is the *timing* of the allocation. As the title suggests, we are concerned with both setting directions and getting there.

The text itself is a mixture of theory and current practice. As John Argenti, who helped introduce planning in Britain, has pointed out; "In corporate planning as in many other disciplines, the theory inspires and informs the practice and the practice confirms and modifies the theory."[1]

Because strategy and planning rely more on skills and wisdom than on techniques and specific knowledge, learning about these aspects of business policy must be done through real or vicarious experience, not through lists of principles. But there is a danger—and a real one—that the unique situations experienced will remain distinct rather than tied together into generalizations useful for the practitioner.

Elements of Business Policy provides the needed integration by (1) describing the most widely used conceptual framework and key variations; (2) placing strategy and planning firmly in perspective, including the role of environmental analysis, organizational structure, and budgeting and control systems; and (3) linking the entire framework to actual practice with illustrative

---

[1]John Argenti, *Corporate Planning: A Practical Guide* (London: George Allen & Unwin, 1968), p. 11.

examples. In addition, a guide to case preparation is included in Appendix A, since often this book may be combined with a selection of case materials for use in MBA or management development programs.

This book owes much to a rich variety of sources. These include business associates, consulting clients, professional colleagues, and legions of students too numerous to mention. However, a few must be singled out. The first is Edmund P. Learned, my business policy teacher, first boss, wise counselor, and constant friend; it is to him that this book is dedicated. Other colleagues at Harvard Business School, where I spent some 15 years as student and professor, contributed stimulating inputs over the years, particularly Kenneth R. Andrews and C. Roland Christensen. Clifford Johnson and the H. A. Johnson Company of Boston, Massachusetts, provided an opportunity to practice what I preached; my years as a consultant and director were invaluable. Joseph W. Nelson of Westinghouse Electric gave the needed verbal and financial prodding to get the writing started, and Dean Floyd A. Bond of The University of Michigan provided an unusually rewarding teaching environment that ensured completion.

My wife, Mimi, took over the strategy and planning of the household while research and writing were in progress and then edited and commented on the manuscript—a much needed task. Still, any errors of omission or commission rest with the author.

David C. D. Rogers

**essentials
of business
policy**

one

THE GENERAL MANAGEMENT POINT OF VIEW

Business policy is concerned with developing the "general management point of view"; this means seeing the key long- and short-term implications of *any* situation, problem, proposal, or decision for the *total* enterprise. The ability to view everything in terms of the whole company is a skill that some managers seem to possess innately, some develop through years of general management experience, some discover through classroom exercises, and some never understand or practice.

The general management point of view demands that the manager sublimate his departmental, functional, or specialist perspective in order to take a balanced, company-wide look.

Practicing a general management role may be done both on the job and in the university setting. In industry, functional managers may be encouraged to understand the cross-functional impact of a decision—how any decision made in any one functional area has an impact on all the other areas and on the company as a whole—through job rotation to other areas. However, short-term shifts in functional area or specialty have limitations: The field may be too complex to learn well and, even if mastered by the transferee, proficiency in a new specialty is not necessarily an indication of general management caliber. Even if there is an opportunity to practice general management skills, the tenure of office is usually too short to evaluate the impact of any strategic decisions made. Therefore, much preparation for an initial or subsequent general manager assignment is done with such vicarious experiences as case studies or simulations, which present complex unstructured situations and demand that participants balance the needs of the conflicting functional areas against each other and those of the total enterprise.

figure one

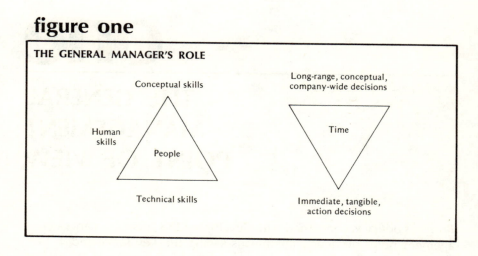

THE GENERAL MANAGER'S ROLE

Conceptual skills

Long-range, conceptual,
company-wide decisions

Human
skills

People

Time

Technical skills

Immediate, tangible,
action decisions

THE HIERARCHY OF MANAGEMENT SKILLS

The role of the general manager may be illustrated with two triangles. (See Figure 1.)[1] At the bottom of the organization are the legions of technicians, specialists, and front line managers hired, retained, and perhaps promoted primarily for their technical competence. Typically, they are concerned with making immediate, tangible, action decisions.

At the top of the pyramid are one or more managers entrusted with the chief executive's job—be it for a profit center, a department, a division, or an entire company. Such executives are responsible for making long-range, conceptual, company-wide decisions; they are heavily dependent on the general management skill of viewing the enterprise as a whole.

In between is the wide band of so-called middle managers, people often promoted for their technical ability but now finding themselves largely concerned with the *human relations* problems of helping people work together toward common goals—goals that they usually did not set or even understand or agree with. As front line managers or lower-level specialists, they were judged on *what* was done, but as middle managers they are judged more on *how* it is done. This is especially diffi-

[1] The classification of managerial ability into technical, human, and conceptual skills was proposed, although with different diagrams, by Robert L. Katz in "Skills of an Effective Administrator," *Harvard Business Review 33,* no. 1 (January–February 1955): 33–42.

cult for middle managers because typically they were hired and promoted on the basis of performing their technical specialties and are completely immersed in their department or functional areas. Small wonder that middle managers—especially those newly promoted from front line positions—sometimes seem to top management to be cursed with myopic vision.

Middle managers must interpret, often with implementing decisions, the conceptual plans made at the top into action terms that are sensible and helpful to those at the bottom of the pyramid. Middle managers must also monitor the actions taken by front line supervisors to see if these actions fit into the mosaic of conceptual, long range, company-wide plans. And they must keep top management informed.

Clearly, the general management point of view is utilized more often at the top of the organizational pyramid; however, its usefulness is not limited to the rarefied atmosphere of the executive suite. Far from it. Many middle managers are in staff positions and work on strategy or planning problems as specialists or as assistants to line managers. The line middle manager needs the general management perspective in order to translate conceptual plans into action effectively (and in so doing often influences or even changes the plans). Many of the operating decisions he makes have strategic implications. Even front line managers, specialists, or new employees fresh out of the university need a general management viewpoint in order to understand the perspective of their bosses. Such an employee can then (1) interpret the instructions he receives from above more broadly, (2) perceive the significance of his own area's potential contribution as corporate priorities shift, and (3) couch the recommendations or proposals he sends upward in terms that make sense to a general manager and are related to his conception of the corporate purpose. The lower level manager may never be a general manager, nor even perform any general management functions; yet with a general management viewpoint he can influence many strategic decisions. In short, managers at all levels of an organization need to develop their general management perspectives in order to be better *subordinates*.

Whatever one's position in an organization, adopting a general management viewpoint is difficult. As Robert L. Katz has pointed out, "What is best for the *total* enterprise is *always* suboptimal from the point of view of an individual unit or function."[2] It is hard to suppress the clear needs of the department or functional area one comes from or knows best in favor of the overall company goal. One needs the judgment to choose, from among conflicting alternatives, what will produce a balanced equilibrium for the company, and one needs a "tough-minded" attitude to overcome the resulting antagonisms. Those with a general management viewpoint realize that they must be satisfied with what is adequate or feasible, while those who are technical specialists want to optimize against a set of limited criteria.[3] Both skills are needed in an organization, although avoiding a conflict is easier in theory than in practice.

Even more difficult, the general management point of view forces a manager to think conceptually in long-range general terms rather than concentrating on immediate, specific actions. For many, this is a difficult shift of gears; acquiring the almost visionary imagination needed is practically impossible for some.

[2] Robert L. Katz, *Cases and Concepts in Corporate Strategy* (Englewood Cliffs, N.J.: Prentice-Hall, 1970), p. 8.

[3] Ibid., pp. 14, 18–19.

two

A CONCEPTUAL FRAMEWORK

Functional managers and students alike bring to a study of business policy a potpourri of discrete bits of knowledge, intuitive wisdom, functional or departmental biases, and isolated experiences. Something is needed to bring a semblance of order out of this chaos. A conceptual framework allows us to organize the pieces into a pattern for subsequent analysis: Conclusions or generalizations may then be deduced. Different frameworks have differing degrees of usefulness, depending on the purpose to which they are to be put. As frameworks change, so may the conclusions or generalizations. A conceptual framework also permits classification of topics. Subtopics such as environmental analysis or perceiving corporate skills or resources may then be fitted into the larger whole and the relationships between such subtopics clarified.

Many practitioners will argue—and quite rightly—that a framework like the one proposed here merely articulates or makes explicit the intuitive approach to business situations developed by the wise businessman or entrepreneur. Indeed, a framework is a poor substitute for intuitive wisdom, but unfortunately, few are blessed with sufficient business intuition. However, this framework is solidly founded on the specific experience of many businesses and businessmen and refined with the help of both practitioners and academicians.

BROAD CONCEPTS: PURPOSE, PROVINCE, AND CHARTER

In most large firms, strategy formulation begins with a broad, qualitative statement of the company's philosophy or *purpose*. This important (but often ignored) statement may be made more specific with the definition of the overall company *province*. A province specifies where the company will concentrate its efforts, in terms of types of customers and particular cus-

5

tomer needs. Even more focused is the *charter*, which broadly defines the product area within which a particular division has been authorized to operate.

Sometimes charters are drawn up for an entire company, in which case they are called corporate images, corporate concepts, business scope or grand designs, and answer the question, What kind of company are we or do we want to become? The image is a very broad statement of the firm's basic objectives or *raison d'être*. In describing the organization's function, the image answers that basic question, What business are we in? The answers may help pinpoint the skills the company has, should develop, or obtain for the future.

Images should indicate how the company defines the scope of its business. By scope is meant the markets and customers served, product mix, range of products (single product niche, horizontal expansion, or diversification with or without some common or synergistic thread), the degree of vertical integration, the geographic coverage, industry position relative to competition, and the basis of competition or "competitive weapons" (such as low cost manufacturing, rapid delivery, innovative R&D, raw material ownership, brand franchise, credit extension, etc.).

A statement of scope or image can be highly useful because, on the one hand, it provides some boundaries for the operations of the firm, and on the other, it prevents some related fields of endeavor from being overlooked. As Theodore Levitt so provocatively asked over a decade ago, "Would the railroad industry be better off today if its management had thought of their business as being not just railroads but transportation?"[1] A *customer* orientation (providing transport) is a much sounder basis for conceptualizing a business than the traditional product orientation (railroads).

For years General Motors seemed to define its business province as "products related to the internal combustion engine," while Lever Brothers claimed to be in the business of "making anything that cleans anything" and Polaroid determined not to stray from the territory embracing "the interaction of light and matter." Such definitions may seem at first glance too broad and vague to be useful; however, they provide considerable focus by ruling out areas of endeavor. Neither Lever Brothers

---

[1] Theodore Levitt, "Marketing Myopia," *Harvard Business Review 38,* no. 4 (July–August 1960): 45.

exhibit one

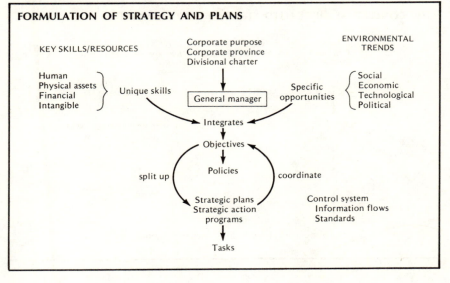

FORMULATION OF STRATEGY AND PLANS

nor Polaroid could venture into the toy business, the steel business, or the food business without a change in image. Even diversified companies search for seemingly elusive synergism; for example, Carborundum, which turns out everything from abrasives to china, likes to point to one common denominator: fiber technology![2]

The definition of a business must be done at the most meaningful level of generalization. For example, a railroad's definition of its business as "transportation" is a start, but in the end the statement should resolve such strategic issues as passenger versus freight, long-haul versus short-haul, unit (or single commodity) versus mixed trains, and so forth. In other words, the image should embrace purpose, province *and* charter.

The roles of these broad concepts, and of the nine specific ones to follow, are diagrammed in Exhibit 1. Planning concepts, in terms of the questions they are supposed to answer, are shown in Exhibit 2.

[2] "Indian Head: The Unsung Success," *Dunn's Review 100*, no. 1, (July 1972): 43.

exhibit two

THE CONCEPTUAL MIX CALLED STRATEGY AND PLANNING

```
Purpose  ⎫
Province ⎬   Functional task: What we are or want to become
Charter  ⎭
   │
   │
   ▼
Objective:        Where we are going, and when we are going to get there
   │
   │
   ▼
         Policy:   How to get there
Strategy ⎧
         ⎨  │
         ⎩  ▼
         Strategic plans:   What to do to reach the objectives
```

THE BUSINESS REVIEW

The foundation for strategy formulation is a thorough, objective, and realistic assessment of the company's or division's past performance and present position. Such a review of strengths and weaknesses makes possible realistic and usable answers to the question, What business are we in? These answers should provide the necessary framework for effective business planning. A typical planning guide issued to top managers in one large company notes:

> Only by defining what you are can you meaningfully describe and plan for what you want to become. . . . The old maxim that "those who fail to learn the lessons of history are doomed to repeat them" applies to business as well as to affairs of state.[3]

A starting point for the business review is to look at the broad measures of performance—growth (sales, profits, assets, owners' equity, number of employees), market share, return on investment—and see what the trends have been, for instance, over the past five years in comparison with other firms in

[3] Westinghouse Electric Corp., *Guide to Business Planning* (Pittsburgh, Pa., 1969), p. 15.

similar markets. A comparison of actual results with prior plans should prompt further questions as to where the company or division excels, what problems remain unresolved, and what seem to be the critical areas or scarce resources.

The results of such a review should not only facilitate explicit, written answers to What business are we in? but also foster some managerial agreement as to what are the *key skills* or *competitive advantage* of the company or division. These key skills or resources will be some combination of people, money, physical assets, and intangibles (such as patent rights or goodwill). Such an examination is concerned not only with inventorying past, present, or future resources but also with specifying which key skills are sufficiently unique in order for the company to capitalize on perceived opportunities in the face of competitive skills. In the jargon of planning, these key skills are often referred to as the "distinctive competence" of the firm.[4]

Unfortunately, the identification of distinctive competence is seldom done explicitly except when searching for diversification opportunities. Then—as will be illustrated in Chapter 3—managers can be very precise as to what their company or division will "bring to the party" and the exact skills or resources required of the acquisition in order to either complement the acquirer's skills or shore up its weaknesses. It seems that managers often need a specific project such as an acquisition to goad them into doing some most necessary self-analysis.

The distinctive competence of a firm is seldom the transitory one of having a unique product or the increasingly widespread characteristic of enjoying sufficient financial resources. One must look at how the product is perceived by the customer relative to competition and the functions performed in taking it to market. The following examples illustrate this point.

1. The Butcher Polish Company, a small regional producer of liquid and paste waxes sold through hardware stores, long had been convinced that its competitive advantage was the high proportion of carnuba rather than synthetics used in its high priced products. During the 1960s, attempts to expand distribution to supermarkets and compete head on with Johnson's Wax and Beacon Wax met with failure. In retrospect, Butcher Polish's real competitive advantage was its distribution channel: the retail hardware dealer's intensive selling of a high margin

[4] This phrase seemingly was coined by Philip Selznick in *Leadership in Administration* (New York: Harper & Row, 1957), pp. 53–55.

item not to be found elsewhere. The shift in distribution destroyed the competitive advantage.

2. Following World War II, a regional chocolate candy manufacturer decided to base future sales growth on company-controlled retail stores rather than on wholesalers and chain stores. The president discontinued his prewar custom of frequent personal visits to wholesalers, dropped the key grocery chain account, and expanded the number of retail outlets from one to seventeen. Management ascribed the high annual level of retail sales—12 pounds per hour per sales clerk—to customers perceiving the quality of hand rather than machine dipping and not being influenced by fancy packages, elaborate displays, or well-known names. Accordingly, the candy was packed in inexpensive paper boxes, promoted solely with small window displays, and priced at half that of other hand dipped. Unfortunately, customer traffic plummeted with the lifting of the sugar ration in 1947 and the return of competitive products. It was only the access to sugar, not the marketing of low-priced hand dipped chocolates, that was the firm's distinctive competence; bankruptcy followed swiftly.

3. Singer, faced with increasing competition in 1958 from higher priced Italian machines and lower priced Japanese ones, no longer perceived its distinctive competence as a sewing machine manufacturer, but as the ability to manage geographically decentralized, comparable operations and build a strong worldwide consumer franchise. Given this perspective, the company greatly expanded the range of white and brown goods marketed through the company stores, even to the extent of letting divisional executives make diversification mistakes as a way of encouraging thinking about products other than sewing machines.[5]

Regarding one's business as satisfying customer needs rather than producing a product may open up new perspectives on resources. For example, the traditional Swiss watch company that saw itself as producing a miniature precision instrument concentrated on engineering and mechanical assembly skills. However, answering the simple question, What is a watch? from the consumer's viewpoint shows that a watch may satisfy a diversity of needs. A watch may be a necessity (for pilots, for example), a gift, an honorarium (after 25 years you may get

[5] "The New Singer Makes a Zigzag Pattern," *Business Week*, November 22, 1969, pp. 58–64.

one), a fad (with Mickey Mouse or a politician's face on the dial), a piece of jewelry, a clothing accessory (with colored bands to match different outfits), a conversation piece (with a crystal back to show off the movement), an extension of one's personality, and so forth. Such a perception of a "watch" enabled Timex and a few others to concentrate on marketing rather than production skills and completely revolutionize the watch industry during the 1960s.

ENVIRONMENTAL ANALYSIS

After the business review comes an assessment of the overall environment and the market, both present and future, in order to pinpoint *specific opportunities*. The general management viewpoint requires starting with an analysis of the broad trends in the economic, social, technological, and political milieus. But the general manager is no mere trend analyzer; rather, he is constantly asking how a particular trend specifically affects his division, competitors, or industry. His final objective is to deduce from that trend a specific product or service opportunity for his division.

Such a process embraces more than most applications of the traditional marketing approach of (1) predicting needs for products or services; (2) pinpointing potential customers; (3) devising strategies for demonstrating, encouraging, and meeting those needs; (4) perceiving competitive reaction to alternative strategies; and (5) formulating a plan of action to market the product or service. The general manager, on the other hand, tries to start with the total environment rather than possible customer needs, and with total corporate skills rather than just those used in marketing.

However, such a global approach poses great problems for a divisional or departmental manager concerned with projecting what will happen to his division's products or services in the marketplace. Translating the effects of such broad economic changes as shifts in the GNP or personal disposable income to the demand for a particular product may seem difficult, if not impossible. Likewise, of what use is a prediction of the social or political climate in the year 2000 or even 1985? The manager has much more immediate problems, such as a profit plan to fill out.

Three approaches help make an environmental analysis relevant:

1. Divisional management must agree on some *explicit assumptions* as to what trends are relevant and when these trends will evolve. For example, in 1959 Lockheed Aircraft set forth the following "major ground rules and assumptions" for *electronics* sales:

Political:	No hot war
	No substantial disarmament
Economic:	Gross National Product—$700 billion in 1970
	Major National Security Expenditures—$57
(all at 1959	billion in 1970
price levels)	Department of Defense Procurement—$19
	billion in 1970
	NASA—$1.6 billion in 1970
Technological:	Continued strong competition between U.S. and USSR
	Evolutionary improvement in reliability and accuracy of missile systems
	U.S. and USSR will prepare for both limited and total war
	Lead time for commercial application of military electronic innovations: 5 years[6]

The relevance of such assumptions for planning projections may be clarified with correlation analysis. For example, cargo transportation demand (ton miles) had a .97 correlation with GNP from 1929–1959.

2. The controllable factors must be distinguished from the uncontrollable ones because by "thinking through the implications of potential change beforehand, the link between environmental change and management response can be clarified and shortened."[7] Some factors, such as the pattern of economic activity, population, or political developments, clearly are not subject to management control. Others—such as industry prices or wages—may be partially influenced by management, while still other factors—such as product quality or marketing and distribution practices—may be controlled by division management to a considerable extent.

[6] Gerald A. Bush, "Prudent Manager Forecasting," *Harvard Business Review 39*, no. 3 (May–June 1961): 58–59.

[7] Westinghouse Electric Corp., op. cit., p. 17.

3. Management can get a clearer picture of product opportunities through the emerging and controversial field of technological forecasting. As will be discussed in Chapter 6, several techniques have emerged, primarily for use in high-technology industries.

Still, there is no question but that much work remains to be done, at both the conceptual and the practical application levels, in the area of opportunity selection. Hence, most corporations start with an in-depth look at internal resources rather than with an environmental analysis, as academic planners would have us do.

SETTING OBJECTIVES

The third step in strategy formulation is the setting of realistic short- and long-range objectives. This process involves the *integration* of specific environmental market opportunities on the one hand with present or potential resources on the other. By integration we mean meshing opportunities and skills—building a mobile that hangs together. Of course, this is an iterative process in that the general manager sees a present or future environmental opportunity and then checks to see if his company has (or can develop or acquire) the skills needed to capitalize on the perceived opportunity. Or, as is more usual if not so theoretically elegant, the manager starts by identifying corporate skills and then seeks appropriate opportunities.

An objective answers the question, *Where* is the company (or division) going and *when* do we want to get there? Involved is a more specific and quantitative restatement of the charter as of a particular time in the future. In multidivision, multiproduct firms, divisional objectives must meet the target earnings levels set by top corporate management, fit within the corporate objectives, and have *measurable* content. Often the more quantitative objectives are called goals.

Viable objectives have several characteristics. First, they should be specific enough to enable a functional manager or a newcomer to know the agreed-upon direction of the company or division as a whole and the direction of any major segment. Second, priorities for both short- and long-run objectives should be established to ensure that undue commitment to short-term results doesn't preclude the attainment of long-term objectives—and vice versa. Third, objectives should not be static; they should be reevaluated constantly in the face of changing opportunities and resources. The integration of opportunities and resources is a moving balance, never static.

Finally, objectives should reflect not only business skills but personal management values, either shared or unique. To the economist, these values focus on risk—gauging the level of risk acceptable to the organization. Acceptable risk levels do vary— the risk with which a manufacturer of high-style women's dresses feels comfortable is obviously quite different from the risk acceptable to the management of a large utility. The values of one's functional area or specialty are hard to shake and only too comfortable to fall back on in times of stress. But especially today, shared management values extend far beyond economic risk or functional background into the sociopolitical realm to make a mockery of the theoretical model of the economic man. These values enter into the formulation of strategy that sets the framework within which the organization will operate.

STRATEGY: THE MIX OF POLICIES AND PLANS

Strategy usually means the mode or plan of action for *allocating scarce resources* to gain a competitive advantage, achieve an objective, and capitalize on a perceived opportunity at an acceptable level of risk.[8] Strategic decisions are those that affect the direction of resource allocation, that determine the future growth of the enterprise. Functional areas—such as marketing, manufacturing, or engineering—should develop separate but consistent substrategies. Clearly, a strategy should be built on the company's or division's unique skills, be designed to minimize competitors' advantages, and be geared to the realities of the situation, not managerial hopes.

Thus defined, strategy really embraces both (1) *policies* and (2) key or strategic *plans*. A policy is a general plan of action that guides employees of a firm in their day-to-day activities toward the company's objectives. It answers the question, *How is the company going to reach its objectives?* Policies may be set consciously or unconsciously by what management says, writes, or does. They must be consistent with objectives and

[8] Broader definitions of strategy include the determination of objectives as well as the mix of policies and key plans that together define the company and its business. The reason for the broader definition is to ensure that the setting of objectives and the choice of policies and plans are integrated and not separated.

with each other, and should be ranked according to their relative importance or to the relative urgency and seriousness of the problems they are designed to solve. A policy such as "we always sell direct" or "we make all our own components" is timeless and remains in effect until revoked.

What is a policy for one echelon may be an objective for a lower one. Without policies, either every decision has to be referred to top management or lower management may make ad hoc decisions that contradict previous decisions, corporate goals, or each other. Once policies are set, management can concentrate on the exceptions; however, formulation of policies does not relieve management of the responsibility for reviewing to ensure that they are still applicable to the constantly changing internal and external environment.

A strategic plan answers the question, *What* has to be done in all functional areas to reach the objectives? A plan is not a forecast. The latter is a prediction of events (such as the weather) over which the planner has little or no control, while a plan specifies the actions to be taken by the planner.[9]

The term *planning* has a variety of meanings, but its broadest *strategic* sense embraces both the process of formulating strategy and the selection of means to implement it. More narrow tactical planning (sometimes called strategic action programs) consists of mapping out a predetermined, coordinated course of action to further the accomplishment of the strategy.

The ascribed differences between strategic and tactical planning are much debated among academicians but are of less interest to the practitioner. For example, management scientist Russell L. Ackoff cites these differences:

1. The longer the effect of a plan and the more difficult it is to reverse, the more strategic it is.
2. The more functions of an organization's activities are affected by a plan, the more strategic it is. . . . (However), a strategic plan for a department may be a tactical plan from the point of view of a division.
3. Tactical planning is concerned with selecting means by which to pursue specified goals . . . normally supplied by a higher level in the organization.

However, Dr. Ackoff notes: "Both types of planning are necessary. They complement each other. They are like the head

---

[9] Preston P. Le Breton and Dale A. Henning, *Planning Theory* (Englewood Cliffs, N.J.: Prentice-Hall, 1961), p. 7.

and tail of a coin: we can look at them separately, even discuss them separately, but we cannot separate them in fact."[10]

More important is the need to differentiate on a day-to-day basis between strategic and operating decisions. As was stated above, strategic decisions are those that affect the direction of resource allocation and thus are concerned with the external effectiveness of the firm. Usually involved in these decisions are such key strategic policy variables as market policy, product policy, distribution policy, and key personnel policy.[11] On the other hand, operating decisions are those that affect the internal efficiency of the firm without materially affecting its future growth. Such decisions embrace such diverse areas as variable cost control, service levels, output, innovations, employee cooperation, bad debt level, and so forth. Improving operating variables usually will increase short-term profits but not guarantee a future.

THE CHARACTERISTICS OF PLANNING

All planning has certain characteristics. First, it is anticipatory, in that it must be done before action is required. Second—and very surprising to many managers—it is concerned with the future implications of current decisions, not with decisions to be made in the future. Rather, the planner examines future alternative courses of action available, makes choices, and thus establishes a frame of reference for current decisions. He then examines how current decisions will affect or limit the scope of future actions.[12] Of course, this does not preclude a timetable for *implementing* today's decisions.[13] Third, planning involves a system of interdependent decisions that cannot be subdivided because of their interrelationship. In the course of planning, earlier decisions must be constantly reviewed in the light of subsequent ones. Fourth, planning is a process with no natural

---

[10] Russell L. Ackoff, *A Concept of Corporate Planning* (New York: Wiley–Interscience, 1970), pp. 4–5.

[11] Katz, *op. cit.*, p. 357.

[12] George A. Steiner, *Top Management Planning* (New York: Macmillan, 1969), p. 6.

[13] As Katz points out: ". . . a strategic plan is a *timed* sequence of *conditional* moves in resources *deployment*. Establishment of *emphasis* and *priorities* is the heart of such a plan. It is essential that a timetable of major moves be established and that the resource requirements and availabilities be clearly spelled out" (p. 356).

conclusion because (1) there is no limit to the amount of re-viewing of previous decisions and (2) both environment and strategy are constantly changing. Hence, one has to "settle for what he has" when action is needed and continually review and update a plan.[14] Fifth, the planning process is always aimed at reaching an implicit or explicit goal. Finally, plans, the results of the planning process, are of a "one-shot" nature, in contrast to the framework of goals and policies for which they are de-termined. Once a plan is put into effect, the general manager starts all over again with a review of environmental opportuni-ties, company skills, alternate strategies, and past plans.

The time span properly covered by a plan is subject to much debate. The minimum time limit may be set by (1) the lead times necessary for research, production, and marketing prepa-ration and (2) the period needed to amortize sunk costs in-volved in the plan—for example, costs of specialized machinery or manpower. The maximum time limit is harder to pinpoint. On the one hand, a definitive plan should extend no further into the future than the period for which it is possible to obtain accurate data and to set concrete, preferably numerical goals (such as a sales forecast). On the other hand, more tentative plans—those that approach dreaming about the future—may be limited only by the sunk planning costs.

The planning function pervades an organization: Everybody plans. In the lower echelons, many people make relatively nar-row, short-range plans or decisions; at the top of the hierarchy, the number of people involved decreases as the breadth of the decisions, the complexity of the variables to be considered, and the time span increase. The problem faced by the middle man-ager is to ensure that all plans at all levels are consistent.

The risk of failing to plan ahead in the face of an uncertain future is that day-to-day decisions may not be consistent with corporate strategy. Yet at some time or other, every executive is convinced that his industry is different—the future is too un-certain to plan ahead. Actually, such comments testify to the usefulness of planning: To the planner, the greater the uncer-tainty, the greater the need to plan. Substituting planning for ad hoc decision making helps ensure that management has agreed on its assumptions as to the future, on what should be done, and on the relative importance of each move or policy.

---

[14] Ackoff, op. cit., p. 3.

exhibit three

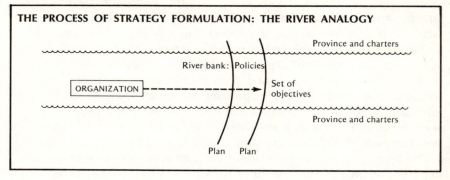

THE PROCESS OF STRATEGY FORMULATION: THE RIVER ANALOGY

a conceptual analogy

The process of corporate strategy formulation described so far may be made clearer with an analogy. If the process is used explicitly, an organization behaves much like a boat going up a river. The province and divisional charters are the surrounding terrain; they influence both the flow and the general direction of the river. The objective is a harbor some distance upstream to be reached by a certain time. The policies are the river banks, which help guide the boat toward the harbor. And like the river banks, policies continue after the goal is reached. They are timeless and must be reviewed as to applicability and consistency whenever new objectives are set. Given this context, a plan is what the crew of the boat must do to further the progress toward the harbor (goal) within the river banks (policies). (See Exhibit 3.)

tactical and profit planning

The entire process of strategy formulation focuses on the most important part of all, tactical plans or strategic action programs that detail how the strategy is to be implemented. This is the action part of planning, indicating what management intends to do *now* and, thus, most subject to division control..

Programs for strategic expenditures, often accompanied by facilities investment schedules, are the detailed heart of planning. Here all the plans are reduced to a series of numbers often involving large commitments of time, people, and money.

This should be the most fully documented part of the entire process, with the expected results and priorities clearly established.

The final link in the planning process is the profit plan, which is a form of quantitative communication. It tells everybody within the company what the future seemingly holds, and informs corporate management of a division's prospects, opportunities, and problems.

Forcing all the written planning documents to be quantified is a useful way of avoiding unnecessary generalities; however, the danger is that the profit plan—and the resulting budgets—will become the sole focus of divisional management attention. For example, during an annual review of divisional long range plans in a large multinational corporation, one prominent divisional manager was asked for the required form showing five-year sales projections by product line for the company and for competition. He looked surprised and asked, "What's that form?" Clearly, his experience had been that, provided he got his budget approved (and met it), he could forget about the back-up planning that the budget was supposed to represent. To him, planning was just budgeting.

FEEDBACK FOR THE PLANNING PROCESS

If the process of strategic planning is to be continuous, with the resulting objectives, policies, and plans constantly updated, there must be a provision for feedback. This feedback is supposed to come via the control system.

It is popular for business writers to draw pretty flow charts showing, for example, how strategic planning leads to tactical planning, which in turn gives rise to implementing decisions, operating decisions, and finally evaluation and replanning. Of course, the control system is shown as the information network linking implementing decisions with operating decisions and both with evaluation. The latter provides input to the replanning process, which completes the loop by influencing both strategic and tactical planning.[15]

A management control system is really a network of *information flows* and *standards* to help management ensure that re-

---

[15] Excellent analyses may be found in Martin K. Star, *Production Management: Systems and Synthesis*, 2d ed. (Englewood Cliffs, N.J.: Prentice-Hall, 1972), pt. I.

sources are obtained and used effectively and efficiently in implementing strategies.[16] As such, it is a mixture of planning and control, and an effective way of analyzing a plan and gauging its completeness is to design an appropriate control system for it.

An effective management control system answers at least three questions: (1) What do I need to know to do my job better within the framework of corporate strategy? (2) How am I performing? (3) How are my subordinates doing? Therefore, management control systems provide information needed for planning and standards for monitoring the plans and evaluating the results. Designing a control system requires pinpointing explicitly those information inputs and standards needed to help management keep operations on track and signal when things are going wrong. It is really an inextricable part of the plan.

Unfortunately, too often the management control system does not provide the all-important feedback needed for effective strategic planning. The chief problem seems to be division of responsibility. For example, formulating strategy may be the province of top-line management, be it a company or a division or functional area. The devising of personal objectives is often part of a management by objectives (MBO) system and the province of the personnel department; the results may bear no relationship to company objectives. The control system may be administered by the controller's department and oriented more to accounting than to planning. And finally, the reward system typically does not emphasize strategic planning and encourage managers to link the control and planning systems in order to implement strategy.

Hence the challenge for the next decade. We know quite a bit about how to formulate strategic plans. The task ahead is to learn how to implement them. The starting point probably will be new and imaginative reward systems that will provide the needed incentive for managers so that they will plan ahead.

---

[16] Robert N. Anthony, *Planning and Control Systems: A Framework for Analysis* (Boston: Harvard Business School, 1965), pp. 16–18. This definition differentiates management control from operational control. The latter is "the process of assuring that specific tasks are carried out effectively and efficiently."

three

SETTING EFFECTIVE OBJECTIVES, POLICIES, AND PLANS

Conceptual frameworks are much easier to articulate than to implement and obtaining real-life and reasonably current objectives, policies, and plans is rather like asking to publish a person's bank statements. Still, a few examples, together with some analysis, should make more explicit and concrete what is really involved in formulating corporate strategy. But perhaps a full appreciation of how hard it is to frame useful objectives may be gained only through experience—by trying to draft some for a company one knows or works for.

The difficulties encountered in framing good objectives and selecting appropriate strategies have spurred a number of innovative approaches. Four are discussed here, including the complete General Electric planning cycle for its new organization concept, Strategic Business Units (SBUs).

CORPORATE PURPOSES

The strategic planning process begins with a broad, philosophic statement of basic purpose. A good example of this for a large, diversified firm is the one put forth by Westinghouse Electric. It reads as follows:

> It is the basic purpose of Westinghouse, in all of its decisions and actions, to attain and maintain the following:
> 1. A continuous high level of profits which places it in the top bracket of industry in its rate of return on invested capital.
> 2. Steady growth in profits, sales volume and high turnover investment at rates exceeding those of the national economy as a whole.
> 3. Equitable distribution of the fruits of continuously increasing productivity of management, capital and labor among stockholders, employees and the public.

4. Design, production and marketing, on a worldwide basis, of products and services which are useful and beneficial to its customers, to society and to mankind.
5. Continuous responsiveness to the needs of its customers and of the public, creating a current product line which is First in Performance and a steady flow of product improvements, new products and new services which increase customer satisfaction.
6. A vital, dynamic product line by continuous addition of new products and businesses and prompt termination of old products and businesses when their economic worth, as measured by their profit performance, becomes substandard.
7. The highest ethical standards in the conduct of all its affairs.
8. An environment in which all employees are enabled, encouraged and stimulated to perform continuously at their highest potential of output and creativity and to attain the highest possible level of job satisfaction in the spirit of the Westinghouse Creed.

These eight points are indivisible. Together, as a unit, they state the fundamental management philosophy of the Westinghouse Electric Corporation.[1]

Some purposes are more specific—but at the risk of being outdated. The following, adopted during happier days by Lockheed Aircraft, provided some definite boundaries and specified some key policies, even if (6) proved impossible in the face of (1) and (5). Certainly, both the objective of being the number one U.S. defense contractor and the key policy of having branded technological products a large proportion of sales still held true in 1974.

The basic purposes of Lockheed are:

1. To be the major company satisfying in the highest technical sense the national security needs of the United States and its allies in space, air, land, and sea.
2. To employ technical resources in meeting the nondefense needs of governments and the requirements of commercial markets.
3. To achieve continuous growth of profits at a rate needed to attract and retain stockholder investment.
4. To recognize and appropriately discharge our responsibilities for the welfare of our employees, the communities in which we do business, and society as a whole.
5. To maintain a large proportion of sales in advanced technical products bearing the Lockheed name.

[1] Westinghouse Electric Corp., *Guide to Business Planning* (Pittsburgh, Pa., 1969), p. 1.

6. To maintain continuity of the enterprise by holding relatively low rates of change of ownership, management and employees.[2]

Purposes typically voice value judgments, though not every corporation expresses lofty principles of social responsibility. For example, Indian Head is refreshing, at least, in reviving good old nineteenth-century capitalism. One set of corporate purposes published for internal purposes began as follows:

OBJECTIVE

The objective of this company *is* to increase the intrinsic value of the common stock.

It is not to grow bigger for the sake of size, nor to become more diversified, nor to make the most or best of anything, nor to provide jobs, have the most modern plants, the happiest customers, lead in new product development, or to achieve any other status which has no relationship to the economic use of capital.

Any or all of these may be, from time to time, a means to our objective, but means and ends must never be confused. Indian Head Mills is in business solely to improve the inherent value of the common stockholder's equity in the company.

SCOPE

The present basis of the company's earning power is a diversified textile business. Continued growth within the textile and related industries is contemplated, in part because the nature of the industry at present seems to offer above average opportunities for expansion.

The company, however, is not committed irrevocably to this industry, particularly if the hazards to be overcome in achieving our objective outweigh the chances of success. There is no ultimate limit to the size of the corporation.[3]

[2] George A. Steiner, *Top Management Planning* (New York: Macmillan, 1969), p. 146.

[3] Reprinted with permission of Indian Head, Inc. The reader should keep in mind that policies change with business conditions and that what was true for Indian Head in 1961 does not necessarily represent company views today. The 1974 version is as follows:

Objective. The objective of Indian Head Inc. is to achieve above average sustained growth in earnings per share as a multi-industry manufacturing and service company operating in the United States and internationally, taking *reasonable* risks and (when appropriate) incurring short-term dilution to achieve such growth.

Approach. Accomplishment of this objective will be based primarily on operating as a diversified company in a number of industries, managed by a career executive in each industry. It will require continually increased operating profits and improved profit performance, while maintaining a satisfactory return on investment based on a blending of growth and

While the nomenclature varies—and almost every company has its own—the business purpose is philosophical rather than quantitative.

Provinces and charters, which define company divisional areas in terms of markets and products, may be stated as a *corporate* image that answers the question, What kind of a business are we or do we want to become? Ralph Cordiner's famous response for General Electric in the early 1950s was:

1. To carry on a diversified, growing, and profitable worldwide manufacturing business in electrical apparatus, appliances and supplies, and in related materials, products, systems and services for industry, commerce, agriculture, government, the community and the home.
2. To lead in research in all fields of science and in all areas of work relating to the business, including managing as a distinct and a professional kind of work, so as to assure a constant flow of new knowledge and of resultant useful and valuable new products, processes, services, methods and organizational patterns and relationships: and to make real the company theme that "Progress Is Our Most Important Product."
3. To operate each business venture to achieve its own favorable customer acceptance and profitable results; especially by planning the product line or services through decentralized operating management, on the basis of continuing research as to markets, customers, distribution channels, and competition, and as to product or service features, styling, price range, and performance for the end user, taking appropriate business risks to meet changing customer needs and to offer customers timely choice in product and service availability and desirability.[4]

The statement continued, but the salient point had been made. In three paragraphs Mr. Cordiner had outlined (1) the

---

stable businesses. Statements of specific objectives and goals for each major business activity throughout the company will be published in writing to all key executives concerned. Such statements will be clear, easily understood, attainable, and compatible with and directly in support of the overall company objective and goals.

Goals. Specifically, our corporate goals are to achieve a 12% compounded annual growth in earnings per share, and a 15% after-tax return annually on average common stock equity, with two-thirds of the earnings growth from existing businesses and one-third from acquisitions financed from cash flow and borrowings.

[4] Ralph J. Cordiner, *New Frontiers for Professional Managers* (New York: McGraw-Hill, 1956), pp. 119–120. Used with permission of McGraw-Hill Book Company.

kind of business in which the world's most diversified corporation was to engage (power generation, power transmission, power distribution, and power consumption); (2) the two key policies (exceptionally extensive R&D and internal management education); and (3) the decentralized organization structure by which the image or broad objectives were to be carried out. It was quite an achievement—sufficient to prompt a spate of objective writing among American companies. The two key policies proved most controversial. GE's management might well claim that the second policy, that of extensive management education, was most important, since for that company planning revolved around manpower. As for the decentralized organization, that was an extreme position from which GE subsequently had to beat a retreat.[5]

CORPORATE OBJECTIVES

For most companies, an objective is a more specific and quantitative restatement of the corporate image as of a particular time in the future: It tells *where* the company or division is going and *when* it wants to get there. Most multiproduct companies retreat into setting overall financial objectives only at the top and leave the business objective writing to divisions or subsidiaries. Single-product companies enjoy no such luxury; top management must tackle this difficult task as an entity. An early (1961) example for a well-known semiconductor company is as follows:

> Remain an ethical manufacturer of semiconductor devices, providing customers with full value and establishing and maintaining a reputation for fair and honest business practices.

> Provide a productive and satisfying work environment for employees, offering career opportunities for personal development and advancement.

> Maximize return on investment, consistent with growth objectives, and operate to protect that investment. The Company has as its objective 15 percent profit before tax and 30 percent return on stockholders' equity and long-term debt. In order to maximize long-term growth and profitability, remain a leader in the semiconductor industry in advanced technology, device development, and engineering.

[5] Company objectives also changed as GE diversified out of the traditional "benign cycle" of power generation to consumption: By 1974, it was a major participant in 13 out of 21 basic industries and involved in all 21; it probably is still the world's most diversified corporation.

Maintain a basic technological capability permitting the Company to develop, produce, and market a specific product within one year. Development is directed toward products which will have a significant market within 2 to 5 years.

Attain a sales volume among the top 5 companies in the semiconductor industry, participating with a broad line of products in approximately 75 percent of all markets, and competing for a minimum of 15 percent in each of the markets.

Participate in industrial, military, and consumer markets. Although emphasis is on the military market, the percentage of industrial business will be increased. Consumer electronic and entertainment devices will be marketed.

Manufacture semiconductor devices in high quantity and at minimum cost consistent with customer quality and volume requirement.

Continue to develop, produce, and market high-performance devices.

Maintain a standard-performance product line which can be produced and marketed at low cost and high volume. This product will employ the technology developed for the high-performance products rather than depend upon new technology.

Develop a product line evolving from discrete components to solid-state circuits, subassemblies, and simple equipment including passive components. These products will include new-type solid-state devices as they begin to displace existing products.

Obtain more contract sales, particularly in areas where contract programs parallel company programs and product plans.

Consider domestic and foreign markets as one integrated world market, with interrelated technical, manufacturing, and marketing opportunities. The Company will exploit the advantages of foreign manufacturing and marketing.

While the reader may think he could do better, these objectives provide some clear focus—and restraints—for the line manager. Development work is closely curtailed in an industry that, at the time, tended to overemphasize R&D. Likewise, the ground rules for market share and breadth of product line are clear; however, a manager would need to know which came first in corporate priorities: breadth, market share, or ROI?

Perhaps the most salient point is that the standard performance line "will include new-type solid-state devices as they begin to displace existing products." The message is clear: Be an aggressive No. 2, not No. 1! This strategy of "runner up" has been remarkably successful for many companies—such as

Celanese versus Du Pont—and success requires an aggressive management to monitor the competitive environment, copy someone else's new product, and rely on low-cost production and quick-reacting marketing to earn an even higher return than the original inventor!

Sometimes objectives are expressed in more general terms and backed up by goals (usually set at the divisional level). One example is that of The Equitable Life Assurance Society—No. 3 in the life insurance industry—and the seemingly innocuous prose of its corporate aims, which holds a great deal of meaning for those involved:

> The Equitable will at all times conduct its affairs in accordance with the highest ethical standards. It will strive for excellence in all of its activities. As a mutual company, The Equitable's operations lead to low cost for its policy and contract owners rather than "profits" in the usual business sense. Nevertheless, its activities will be conducted with the same emphasis on efficiency, productivity, and competitive superiority as if it were in business for profit.

CORPORATE PURPOSES

The Equitable's primary purpose is to provide sound, equitable, and economical protection against financial hazards arising from variations in health and length of life. The Equitable carries out this purpose principally through the traditional role of risk-bearing life and health insurance and annuities together with the investment of associated funds, and also through the provision of related products and services that enhance the ability of people to protect themselves. Continuing responsiveness to the nation's evolving economic, social, and legal structure is indispensable in carrying out this purpose.

The Equitable is essentially a public service institution engaged in a most important human activity—providing financial security for individuals and families. It thus enhances peace of mind and confidence, assures a measure of financial independence, and contributes significantly to the social good.

In addition to its contribution to the nation's well-being flowing from the accomplishment of its primary purpose, The Equitable takes a strong part in helping to improve the quality of life in America. Through its employment practices, investment policies, the corporate contributions, and the activities of its people, The Equitable supports national and community efforts in such matters as providing opportunities for the disadvantaged, advancement of education, health and welfare programs, and improvement of the environment.

The Equitable engages in ancillary activities in order to enhance and support its business and social purposes. Special emphasis is accorded those activities and opportunities for which The Equitable is particularly qualified because of the experience and capabilities of its people, and the role it plays in the nation's social and economic structure.

CORPORATE OBJECTIVES

The Equitable's primary objective is to increase continuously the degree of fulfillment of its corporate purposes. To do so, it pursues the following objectives.

The Equitable's growth objective is to grow in a planned and orderly manner at the maximum rate subject to considerations of profitability, relative prices, and social purposes. Like most organisms of life, a business is unlikely to be vigorous and successful if it does not grow. Enterprising employees and agents are more readily attracted to a growing organization because there is a greater opportunity for personal development and associated rewards. Unit costs of doing business can more readily be kept under control in an expanding situation. A large and growing organization is usually better able to assume some of the obligations of the greater society of which it is a part and thereby contribute to the general well-being. This is not to say the largest firm is always the best; frequently that is not the case. But real growth has desirable attributes even for the largest or the best.

The Equitable's investment objective is to manage the funds entrusted to it so as to produce the maximum rate of return subject to considerations of quality, liquidity, and social purposes. In carrying out its business purpose, The Equitable undertakes services and substantial liabilities for benefits running far into the future, and in exchange receives a large in-flow of funds. The funds accumulated in the process are invested in debt obligations and equities backed by the assets and earnings power of thousands of individuals and corporations. These funds provide a source of capital for the nation's economy and for the development, use, and preservation of the nation's resources, and they are invested in ways that assure availability of the funds when needed to provide promised benefits . . .

CORPORATE GOALS

In furtherance of its growth objective, The Equitable will continue to establish consistent long- and short-range goals in terms of carefully selected and expressly defined indicators of growth for the different lines of business and major activities, coupled with equally well selected and defined constraints. The Equitable will also continue to establish appropriate goals for its other corporate objectives.

Subordinate and supportive goals and the necessary strategies, plans and budgets, programs, and projects will continue to be developed by those responsible for each part of the organization and will be fully communicated. If review and analysis of supportive plans show that the corporate goals are either unreasonably high or low, the corporate goals will be modified in order to achieve consistency throughout the hierarchy of goals.[6]

The thoughtful reader may have noted several points. For example, the first paragraph discusses the difficult position of a mutual company, with responsibilities to current policyholders often conflicting with managerial desire for growth. In fact, owing to the heavy initial costs, too rapid growth in terms of new policies means substantial book losses! After all, from the *current* policyholder's viewpoint, The Equitable could well concentrate on service and sell no new policies at all.

Even more difficult is the position on the "national well-being." In insurance circles this is interpreted to mean supporting price stability, since traditional or ordinary life insurance has fixed dollar payouts. But what if inflation is here to stay? Think of the impact on capital sources if the *largest* supplier of debt capital starts to require equity participation in *all* long-term debt instruments (as the John Hancock did in late 1968). And what about the payoff, if not in predetermined dollar amounts? How does one explain a variable policy to the uninitiated? All these questions—and many more—lay behind the intense discussion surrounding publication of The Equitable's corporate aims.

Many salesmen might view the revised statement as a threat to their jobs. Just selling variable annuities meant qualifying as a registered representative with the SEC—a most difficult task for some. Any shift to term or variable life meant a fraction of the ordinary-life commissions, while continued emphasis on group policies required a few, highly skilled negotiators, not a mass of door-to-door salesmen.

The investment paragraph talks about the large inflow of funds, and the implementing plans predict that 65 percent of the individual policies will continue to be whole or ordinary life (a combination of death insurance plus forced savings that level out the premiums). But should policyholders' confidence in the dollar falter, savings will go elsewhere. Then The Equi-

[6] Reproduced by permission of The Equitable Life Assurance Society of the United States.

table would need stock market portfolio analysts instead of its nationwide mortgage and long-term investment organization.

Fortunately, the purpose makes sense until at least 1980; while insurance companies (including Equitable) are rapidly entering the casualty field through acquisition, and banks are entering the insurance field, the marketing of variable life poses many problems and the day when an insurance company offers complete financial services (from mutual funds to commercial banking to personal budgeting to estate planning and tax consulting) seems still a bit removed.

Looking back over the whole statement, one might wonder what skills or resources The Equitable has should whole life not continue as a viable contract. The purposes talk about "ancillary activities"; as of 1974, these included such ventures as relocation services (purchase of existing homes, search for new homes, and appraisal); a real estate investment trust; and a computer services company. Without the cash flow from whole life, The Equitable becomes a large processor of paper and its skill the ability to develop and operate computer-based paper work systems. As a way of "dipping one's toes in the water," The Equitable is administering Medicare programs for several southwestern states and has bid on the job of servicing all the health and welfare programs of the City of New York.

problem areas

Even with the preceding examples, two difficult challenges of objective writing stand out: (1) making the objectives sufficiently specific to be useful to operating management and (2) spelling out the implications for each area of the company.

The problem of specifying objectives is obvious to anyone who has been involved in writing or using them. What is needed is a *future description* of the company or business unit sufficiently detailed for an outsider or departmental manager to see where the unit is going and what his role should be. The solution is to include all the key policies in order to "flesh out" the objective. For example, the one area in which companies are specific is diversification objectives. The business press is replete with public statements describing in detail the acquisition objectives of Textron and other conglomerates and spelling out the kinds of companies needed and the criteria used to judge the prospects. An illustration of a policy-laden statement of Textron's diversification criteria is shown as Exhibit 1.

Showing the implications of an objective is possible if quantified goals or strategies are included that specify the cost of the resources required, the possible payoffs in financial terms, and the statistical probability of success. The use of relevant costs in contribution analysis is a most useful tool in this regard.[7] Even published statements are being quantified. For example, Textron, Inc.'s 1973 Annual Report began as follows:

TEXTRON'S CONCEPT AND OBJECTIVES

Textron is founded on the principle of balanced diversification, designed on the one hand to afford protection against economic cycles and product obsolescence and on the other to provide a means for participating in new markets and new technologies. The key elements are balance and flexibility in a rapidly changing world.

The primary goal is superior performance on a continuing basis. This includes above average growth in earnings per share and in dividends.

Textron seeks to be distinctive in its products and services: distinctive as to technology, design, service and value. Superior performance rests upon excellence and quality.

Textron operations are conducted through a number of Divisions in five Groups—Aerospace, Consumer, Industrial, Metal Product and Creative Capital. Each Division carries on its business under its own well-known name with its own organization. Management philosophy is based on decentralization of day-to-day operations coupled with centralized coordination and control to assure overall standards and performance.

There are three priorities: People development. Internal growth. Extending the Textron concept into new areas.

To achieve the goal of superior performance, the specific targets for the ten-year period ending in 1982 are:

> Sales expansion at an average compound rate of 8%, to $3.5 billion by 1982. Net income growth at an average compound rate of 10%, to $200 million by 1982. Earnings per share up at an average compound rate of 10%, to $6.00 by 1982.

POLICIES

Including explicit, consistent policy statements in a strategy helps avoid hasty ad hoc decisions that are incompatible with

---

[7] Readers not comfortable with analyzing and projecting financial statements and with the useful tool called contribution analysis might refer to the author's concise review, *The Manager's Guide To Finance and Accounting* (Ann Arbor, Mich.: Landis Press, 1972).

exhibit one

EXAMPLES OF DIVERSIFICATION POLICIES GIVEN IN A PUBLIC SPEECH

The following excerpts are from a 1966 address by Charles Chapin, assistant treasurer of Textron, about the policy guidelines used by Textron in diversifying from a textile company to a major conglomerate during the 1950s and 1960s.

. . . In its diversification program, Textron has remained entirely in manufacturing-type businesses. Even though we have an extremely wide spread of interests, the management techniques, standards of performance, and measurements of the use of capital are basically similar from one manufacturing business to another. . . .

Textron prefers its divisions to be the leading company in a small or medium-size industry, rather than a minor factor in a major industry. . . .

Textron classifies its acquisitions in two general categories: these are either a new product or a product line-type acquisition. To be considered as a new product acquisition, the company must have a sales volume of $20 million or more and be in a field in which we do not participate. We have found that a company should have about this sales volume or more to support a proper staff of people to operate the company under our autonomous, decentralized, profit-center type of organization. Textron does not staff a unit when it is acquired, so it is essential that we acquire good management that will remain.

A product-line acquisition can be almost any size but it must complement one of our present divisions. In a product-line acquistion, we will accept weak management situations or other problems if we feel the division into which it would fit can assimilate the acquisition and solve the problem. It is in this type of acquisition that you most often can expect to achieve the synergistic effect of making 1 and 1 equal to 3 that is so widely publicized in acquisition circles.

When a company is first proposed to us as a potential acquisition, we review it to see whether it meets a number of basic criteria and any company we do acquire must have four characteristics:

1. It must be a manufacturing company.
2. It must be able to meet our return on investment and profit margin standards.
3. It must increase our earnings per share.
4. Its growth potential must be equal to or better than what we expect for Textron as a whole.

If it is a new product-type acquisition—then, we also want the company to be a leader in a small industry and have a product line that has one of or a combination of the following strong attributes: proprietary products, a patent position, a solid position in its field due to its marketing abilities, be in an industry with a high cost of entry, have a product that requires a special manufacturing skill and/or is a product which has a high technological content. The product line should also be of unquestionable quality. In our opinion, quality products are of paramount importance and in the long run are the only kind we can manufacture if we are to achieve the consistent profitable future growth for which we are planning.

In a product line acquisition, the company must be able to add something to the division into which it will fit. There can be a wide range of factors involved such as a complementary product line, a sales force, a manufacturing facility, an entry into a new market, a new technology, and/or integration of manufacture, but in the final analysis it must add something to the Textron division that will absorb it. Incidentally, the division management of Textron must also really want the acquisition as once we have acquired it then the new acquisition becomes the responsibility of the division. . . .

If a proposed acquisition meets these general tests, then we proceed with a more careful review of the situation and with what its impact on Textron would be. In the financial area, we determine first of all if and how we can achieve at least a 25% pretax return on the capital we would have to invest. . . . [If the projected return would be under 25 percent, Textron would investigate the possibilities of either raising earnings or cutting the investment base to meet the stated criteria.]

On the operational side, we make a careful industry study to be sure that there is a basic underlying growth of an above average nature which will continue without wide cyclical fluctuation, and that the industry serves a fundamental economic need in world markets. This need can range from consumer demands for higher living standards to machinery to reduce direct manufacturing costs. . . .

As mentioned earlier, management is the most important ingredient in a company and in an acquisition we must be sure that we are acquiring high-grade, professional, capable management which will stay after we have acquired their company. In fact, we want them to enter our family of employees with a spirit of enthusiasm and ambition that matches our own. When we feel that there would be a serious personality conflict or room for disagreement—then, we would not make the acquisition. We also carefully define prior to acquisition what [each] key person's responsibilities will be after the acquisition so all important people involved are well informed in advance as to what their respective positions are. As evidence of our care in this regard is the fact that we have never unwillingly lost any key people after an acquisition, except through retirement or illness.

SOURCE: Reproduced by permission of Textron, Inc.

corporate goals. Unlike the corporate goals, these statements have no time limits—for example, "we always sell direct."

The marketing policies for Indian Head Mills started as follows:

MARKETING POLICIES

1. Do not sell ahead at a loss.
2. No products are to be kept in the line which cannot be made to provide a profit. It is impossible to make enough on the winners to overcome losses on losers. *It is not the policy of the company to have a complete line in order to keep a customer happy or provide extra service or convenience.* Let competitors have the losers.
3. Do not build inventory without reasonable expectation of marketability. If orders are not in hand or reasonably foreseeable, production is to be curtailed. Do not produce inventories as a cushion for customer service. Inventories are produced to make a profit.
4. Keep all marketing people informed what inventory costs (real costs, not standards) relative to selling prices, including the cost of carrying slow-moving or unsaleable merchandise.
5. Keep the corners swept out. It is company policy to have at least one annual housecleaning as an exercise in shrinking capital investment to minimum levels, and to get rid of unprofitable or slow-moving merchandise. More frequent inventorying is highly recommended.[8]

They are clear, if unusual.

An unusually complete example of a company's marketing policies is shown as Exhibit 2, together with the introduction to the complete policy manual. The consistency of the policies is worth noting.

PLANS

Obtaining good actual examples of plans is most difficult because they are concerned with coordinated *action* decisions to be taken in all functional areas to accomplish the objectives within policy guidelines. Revealing plans tells too much about either the shortcomings of the process or what the management intends to do.

However, one can illustrate the process with hypothetical examples or ones drawn from highly regulated industries, such

[8] Reprinted with permission of Indian Head, Inc. The reader should keep in mind that policies change with business conditions and that what was true for Indian Head in 1961 does not necessarily represent company views today.

as insurance or utility companies. (They are required to make public so much information that they are not averse to releasing their actual plans.) Three examples should suffice:

Motorola's planning system in the mid-1960s is a good example of a structured approach with a format designed to force quantified, specific plans, assignment of responsibility, and follow-up. The example given in Exhibit 3 illustrates the problems of nomenclature. What Motorola called "goals" at a *functional division* level (the physical distribution department of the Business Machines Division) were often really plans—especially when viewed at the corporate level. (Nos. 4.1–4.3, 5.1, 5.3, and 6.2 are clearly in this category.)

The Equitable Life Assurance Society's computer planning model illustrates (1) how planning should be done around a key skill (in this case, sales force or agent manpower), (2) how a model output can be used to influence change, and (3) how planners may utilize the computer for ease of projecting. Excerpts from the 1971 and 1972 printouts, shown in Exhibit 4, clearly demonstrate the effects of shifting assumptions about (1) the number of salesmen, retention rate, and productivity projected by the agency department and (2) the introduction of new products, such as variable life. Chapter 4 will discuss the role of the computer in planning.

a summarized example of strategic planning

Airlines have long been a leader in formal planning and, because it is a state-owned corporation, British Airways[9] has been willing to discuss the substance as well as the format of its plan. The 240-member planning organization carries out extensive strategic and operational planning with the corporate plan projected five years.

The planners started with setting the corporate purpose and objectives.[10] Constrained by the 1971 Aviation Act from manufacturing airframes or engines, management decided British Airways was not merely a carrier or even in the air transport business; rather, its purpose was "to provide for the travel of

[9] Created to be responsible for the affairs of BEA and BOAC as of April 1972.

[10] Stephen F. Wheatcroft, "Integrating British Airways," *Journal of General Management 1*, no. 2 (1973–1974): 23–36. Written by the former Group Planning Manager, this is a concise description of a very complex process; for a more critical discussion, see "The Stately Merger of Britain's State Airlines," *Business Week*, August 25, 1973, pp. 36–37.

exhibit two

INTRODUCTORY COMMENTS TO A FOOD COMPANY'S POLICY BOOK

As the individual grows and matures, he accumulates knowledge, experience, and principles which guide and regulate his thinking and his actions.

A group of individuals, however, has no "group brain" which automatically determines the behavior of all its members. Therefore, if the group is to think and act as a unit and to have group life and force and meaning, some way must be found to achieve coordination.

Policy supplies that influence.

If policy is absent there is a lack of leadership, confusion, disorganization and dispersion of strength. When it is present and effective the organization will have a coherent point of view and the energies of many people will be fused into a unit for effectively achieving common objectives.

Sound policy has two characteristics:

—It is fundamentally stable.
—It operates as a creative force, not as a brake on progress.

Our company has had policies and principles which have changed gradually with the continued growth of the company and with varying conditions. As the organization grows larger, it becomes increasingly important that these policies be clearly and completely understood so that:

—The efforts of the entire organization will be directed uniformly towards accomplishing our objectives.
—We may present a united front in dealing with outside groups.
—We will have a strong framework within which to delegate responsibility and authority.

Policy must reckon with new circumstances. No policy should outlive by one minute the specific conditions to which it is adapted. As times change policies should be changed. Policy must be realistic. The day when it ceases to bear directly on the prevailing operation it ceases to have value as a policy and is nothing more than a habit.

Change of policy should, however, be a considered thing—not subject to whim or quick decision because the opportunity of the moment is tempting. There must always be indisputable evidence that the time for change is at hand.

Suggestions for changes in these policies, supported by sound reasons, will always be welcome and will be given careful consideration. Until such changes are made, all members of the organization should conduct their activities within the framework of these policies.

MARKETING POLICIES

The Marketing Division is concerned with forecasting the Company's sales requirements on a realistic basis, and it has the responsibility for the orderly liquidation of the inventory at such prices and promotional levels as will produce maximum profits to the Company, while maintaining consumer and trade goodwill through honest and reliable advertising, selling, and service.

market on a planned basis

It is the policy of the Company:

To carefully plan the orderly liquidation of the pack.

The Marketing Division initiates the annual Profit Plan by indicating the quantities of product which can be profitably marketed in the ensuing year.

Because we are dealing in agricultural commodities, the actual supply may vary widely from the budgeted supply. This necessitates a revised determination by management as to the quantity of each commodity to be marketed prior to the ensuing pack. Then a final marketing plan is developed which takes into consideration the relative movement and profit at various levels of price and promotion.

price for profit

It is the policy of the Company:

To price our products so as to yield the maximum profit over the long term.

This means that products with distinctive premium-quality characteristics are priced so as to more than recover the cost of developing and sustaining such products, and that the inevitable by-products are priced competitively so as to yield the maximum profit to the Company over the long term.

price consistent with planned movement

It is the policy of the Company:

To price consistent with the planned movement of the product.

Recognizing the fact that price affects movement, it is the Company's policy to price at such levels as will, together with planned advertising and promotion, maintain movement at the planned rate.

recognize competition in pricing

It is the policy of the Company:

To price each item with full awareness of that item's competition.

Recognizing our leadership in the commodities we pack, our price will influence, to a large extent, competitive prices. Nevertheless, our price on each item must take cognizance of what competitive reaction will be.

guarantee price against decline

It is the policy of the Company:

To guarantee our prices to the trade against our own decline.

We recognize our responsibility to maintain such prices as will provide necessary consumer purchases; to price so as to maintain shelf velocity.

Our guarantee permits buyers to take deliveries of adequate quantities for aggressive merchandising programs without fear of loss in the event of a negative price change.

EXHIBIT TWO *(Continued)*

promote consistent with planned movement

It is the policy of the Company:

To promote the movement of our items to assure the orderly liquidation of the pack.

Along with price, promotion affects movement. It is the Company's objective to strike a balance between price and promotion that will yield the greatest profit to the Company consistent with the planned movement.

emphasize company brand names

It is the policy of the Company:

To place marketing emphasis on Company brands and most especially Company premium-quality brands.

There is no point in offering the consumer a better package of food unless such packages can be universally recognized and identified. It is our policy, therefore, to promote and feature Company premium-quality brands.

recognize the function of distributor labels

It is the policy of the Company:

To recognize the function of distributor labels and to integrate the same into the basic scheme of marketing the Company's products.

Distributor labels hold an important position in the total marketing scheme as a means whereby store loyalty can be built through the offering of value merchandise under the distributor franchise. The Company actively solicits distributor label business where such will dispose of predictable quantities of merchandise which management has determined will serve to promote the long-term profitability of the Company's operations.

maintain constant and reasonable distributor stocks

It is the policy of the Company:

To maintain constant and reasonable supplies of our items in distributor hands.

Constant supplies are now a mandatory operating rule for aggressive distributors. This makes it incumbent upon us to have a continuing, reasonable supply of merchandise available upon demand by distributors.

An out-of-stock situation at retail means lost sales; the regaining of usual shelf facings is difficult. The Sales Department strives continually to keep distributors and their retail outlets stocked and in business month in, month out, with our brands.

advertise consistently

It is the policy of the Company:

To make funds available for advertising on a consistent basis.

The Company maintains a consistent advertising program year after year, regardless of temporary market conditions. Advertising is a powerful force, but it cannot be turned off and on and maintain its effectiveness. The consumer picture is an ever-changing parade, with old families dropping out and new families being added to the picture daily.

co-ordinate advertising with promotional activity

It is the policy of the Company:

To co-ordinate the advertising with promotional activity so that there is a series of events which creates special consumer demand and alerts and stimulates the trade to display and feature our brands.

Recognizing that advertising reinforced by retail activity increases the efficiency of the advertising, we try to coordinate the two activities.

distribute advertising impressions nationally

It is the policy of the Company:

To distribute advertising impressions on a national basis with supplemental efforts in local heavy-buying areas and in areas where our brand position needs strengthening.

The media which the Company selects are those which reach the widest segment of our most ideal prospects, and concentrate in opportunity and problem areas.

maintain advertising integrity

It is the policy of the Company:

To maintain complete honesty in our advertising.

Advertising integrity is a *must* which pays off over the years to establish the character of our Company in the consumers' minds.

It does not preclude advertising the fun in the eating of our products, nor does it stilt or prevent new dramatic approaches to the advertising operation. It does convey the over-all "good business" philosophy of management.

make the agency a part of the company

It is the policy of the Company:

To regard the advertising agency as a business affiliate with access to the pertinent facts, figures, and policies of the Company.

This policy recognizes the fact that, to be of greatest benefit to us, the agency must be intimately familiar with our operations, products, markets, and our strong and weak points.

This familiarity helps the agency to determine which is the best possible usage for our advertising dollars.

· · ·

SOURCE: Earl L. Bailey, *Formulating the Company's Marketing Policies* (New York: The Conference Board, 1968), pp. 42, 44–46.

exhibit three

MOTOROLA, BUSINESS MACHINES DIVISION (HYPOTHETICAL)
DISTRIBUTION   OBJECTIVES AND GOALS   AUGUST 1, 1965 (DATE)

OBJECTIVES	GOALS	TARGET DATE	PRIME RESPONSI-BILITY	STATUS AS OF ——— (DATE)
1. Achieve and maintain an annual average rate of Return on investment of 27%.	1.1 Over-all financial results:ª 1.2 Acquire a business whose products may be efficiently and effectively distributed throughout existing branches and dealers and which may be expected to provide $10,000,000 additional sales by 1970.	1966 1967 1968 1969 1970 1-1-68	Division Manager Division Manager	
2. Maintain and improve the effectiveness of and market penetration gained through existing sales branches.	2.1 For the New Orleans, Dallas and Cincinnati branches, establish detailed written plans for the establishment of their sales, market penetration and expense goals.	11-1-65	Branch Managers who are involved	
	2.2 Establish a program whereby each branch manager will make a formal annual presentation extending his five-year plans one additional year into the future, reporting on accomplishments of the past year (vs. plan) and emphasizing: —manpower needed at all levels —training and/or recruitment plans —market penetration —expense ratios.	1-1-66	Field Sales Manager	
3. Use existing customer acceptance and image of the Motorola brand in the business machines field in introducing new products to the market.	3.1 Have all the division's products conform to the standard styling program.	3-1-66	Chief Engineer	

OBJECTIVES	GOALS	TARGET DATE	PRIME RESPONSI-BILITY	STATUS AS OF ———— (DATE)
4. Establish and maintain adequate distribution in markets west of the Mississippi.	4.1 Improve market penetration in markets west of the Mississippi (relative to the Eastern part of the country) as follows:			
	—70% of East US penetration	1965	Western U.S.	
	—75% of East US penetration	1966	Field	
	—80% of East US penetration	1967	Sales	
	—85% of East US penetration	1968	Manager	
	—90% of East US penetration	1969		
	—95% of East US penetration	1970		
	4.2 Establish, in Salt Lake City, a combination local factory branch and distribution warehouse to serve Western US branches and dealers with both equipment and parts.	3-1-67	Western U.S. Sales Manager	
	4.3 Open factory branches (replacing dealers) as follows:			
	—San Francisco, Calif.	2-1-66	Manager	
	—Portland, Oregon	10-1-66	of	
	—Salt Lake City, Utah	3-1-67	Branches & Western U.S. Sales Manager	
5 To the maximum extent which rising sales volume will support, broaden our program of branch office representation in the major metropolitan markets.	5.1 Open additional factory branches, (replacing dealers) as follows:			
	—2 branches (Minneapolis and Memphis)	1965	Manager of Branches	
	—5 branches (Portland, St. Louis, Wash. D.C., Dayton, San Francisco)	1966		
	—3 branches (Louisville, Salt Lake City, Omaha)	1967		

EXHIBIT THREE *(Continued)*

OBJECTIVES	GOALS	TARGET DATE	PRIME RESPONSI- BILITY	STATUS AS OF ——— (DATE)
	5.2 Complete and insti- tute a program for selling complete lines of Motorola branded ribbons and tapes through our branches.	3-1-66	Assistant Sales Manager	
	5.3 Have these supplies account for 5% of sales of branches.	Year 1968	Assistant Sales Manager	
6. Establish and maintain a pro- gram which will provide all of our customers with prompt, reason- ably priced, and reliable mainte- nance and service on their Motorola machines.	6.1 Have all existing branches meet minimum service capability standards.	6-1-66	National Service Manager and Manager of Branches	
	6.2 Increase the percent- age of dealers who must meet these standards, as follows:			
	—Dealers doing 70% of our dealer billings	12-31-65	National Service Manager and National Sales Manager	
	—Dealers doing 80% of our dealer billings	12-31-66		
	—Dealers doing 85% of our dealer billings	12-31-67		

OBJECTIVES	GOALS	TARGET DATE	PRIME RESPONSI-BILITY	STATUS AS OF ———— (DATE)
7. Establish and maintain a factory, branch and dealer distribution organization . . . [to sell] complementary lines of products.	7.1 Appoint Product Sales Managers for each product line, to work with regional and branch managers, and to see that the product line gets constant attention.	6-1-66	National Sales Manager	
	7.2 For each product line, prepare a sales plan which will assure constant attention in the field.	12-31-66	Product Sales Managers	

Sales 000,000	Margin %	Profits 000,000	Turnover	ROI %
32.5	9.5	3.1	2.1	20
37.0	9.5	3.5	2.1	20
42.0	9.1	3.6	2.2	20
50.0	10.0	5.0	2.2	22
60.0	12.5	7.5	2.4	30

SOURCE: Reproduced with permission of Motorola, Inc.

exhibit four

**EXAMPLE OF A COMPUTER-BASED FORMAL PLANNING SYSTEM:
THE EQUITABLE LIFE ASSURANCE SOCIETY**

Long-range planning is especially vital in the life insurance industry because as much as 90 percent of the current income for a typical company is on the books as of the start of the year. Management cannot wait until results falter to take corrective action to ensure future profits.

On the other hand, life insurance lends itself to quantitative planning because the key variables are not numerous, can be isolated, and may be forecast with considerable accuracy. Computer programs usually start with an agency model that predicts sales force productivity and then uses the output as the revenue input for an individual life operations model. Selections from two computer runs done by The Equitable should be illustrative of both the approach and the importance of carefully selecting and forecasting variables.

THE INITIAL RUN, 1971

YEARS					1966	1967	1968	1969	1970
1971	1972	1973	1974	1975	1976	1977	1978	1979	1980

SALES MANPOWER PLAN (1970 BASE)

I. Management Base and Recruitment Capacity, 1966–1980

Starters (new agents)

					1797	1893	2143	2348	2404
2471	2500	2600	2700	2800	2900	3000	3100	3200	3300

II. Retention Rates for New Agents or Starters (%)

A Class (agents hired during year)

					66.8	68.9	68.0	63.6	62.2
60.0	60.0	60.0	60.0	60.0	60.0	60.0	60.0	60.0	60.0

B Class (new agents, second year)

					35.2	29.9	32.2	28.6	24.5
26.5	27.0	27.5	28.0	28.5	29.0	29.5	30.0	30.5	31.0

C Class (new agents, third year)

					30.3	23.1	22.4	19.0	18.6
17.0	17.5	18.0	18.5	19.0	19.5	20.0	20.5	21.0	21.5

D Class (new agents, fourth year)

					27.8	24.2	18.1	17.0	15.2
15.0	15.5	16.0	16.5	17.0	17.5	18.0	18.5	19.0	19.5

ESF (experienced sales force)

					86.7	87.1	87.7	83.0	90.0
91.0	91.0	91.0	91.0	91.0	91.0	91.0	91.0	91.0	91.0

III. Population, 1966–1980

Total Agency Force (excluding retirees)

					5968	5829	5929	5470	5469
5561	5720	5928	6162	6419	6696	6993	7310	7646	8001

YEARS	1966	1967	1968	1969	1970	1971	1972	1973	1974	1975	1976	1977	1978	1979	1980

IV. Productivity, 1966–1980 (per capita production credits)[a]

Category	1966	1967	1968	1969	1970	1971	1972	1973	1974	1975	1976	1977	1978	1979	1980
A Class	1870	1687	1704	2025	2575	2600	2756	2921	3097	3282	3479	3688	3909	4144	4393
B Class	4995	5082	4949	5284	5824	6000	6360	6742	7146	7575	8029	8511	9022	9563	10137
C Class	5501	5616	5576	5903	6231	6400	6784	7191	7623	8080	8565	9079	9623	10201	10813
D Class	5878	5720	6064	6206	6659	6700	7102	7528	7980	8459	8966	9504	10074	10679	11320
ESF	6023	6305	6727	7956	8319	8600	9116	9663	10243	10857	11509	12199	12931	13707	14530

V. Total Production Credits, Agency Expenses (thousands of dollars)

Category	1966	1967	1968	1969	1970	1971	1972	1973	1974	1975	1976	1977	1978	1979	1980
Total production credits	33569	33368	34578	37180	39565	41160	44539	48482	53003	58118	63873	70361	77657	85839	94995
Percent yearly increase	4.3	−.6	3.6	7.5	6.4	4.0	8.2	8.9	9.3	9.7	9.9	10.2	10.4	10.5	10.7
Total agency department expenses	45718	47241	52186	60514	65600	70684	76268	82865	90204	98510	107851	118241	129938	143103	158073

VI. Individual Life—Net Income from Operations

The effects of these and other changes on individual life, which is the backbone of the company, are translated into projected income statements and changes in balance sheet accounts:

Net Income from Operations (millions of dollars)

Category	1966	1967	1968	1969	1970	1971	1972	1973	1974	1975	1976	1977	1978	1979	1980
Net Income	21.1	20.6	16.6	13.0	9.9	10.4	10.6	12.3	12.2	9.5	5.6	1.3	−3.9	−8.9	−13.9

A SPRING 1972 RUN

A redefinition of both retention and productivity rates dramatically changed the number of starters needed and the results. The following examples illustrate the opportunity to ask "what if?" strategy questions.

[a] A production credit is approximately the *first-year* dollar commissions; it is the standard output or productivity figure for the industry.

EXHIBIT FOUR *(Continued)*

YEARS

1962	1963	1964	1965	1966	1967	1968	1969	1970	1971
1972	1973	1974	1975	1976	1977	1978	1979	1980	1981

I. Management Base and Recruitment Capacity, 1962–1981

Starters

1480	1270	1634	1721	1797	1893	2143	2348	2404	2482
2572	2700	2835	2975	3124	3280	3444	3616	3796	3986

II. Retention Rates, 1962–1981

A Class

70.1	65.4	71.1	71.4	66.8	68.9	68.0	63.6	62.2	55.8
60.0	60.0	60.0	60.0	60.0	60.0	60.0	60.0	60.0	60.0

B Class

36.0	39.9	44.0	42.5	35.2	29.9	32.2	28.6	24.5	25.7
26.9	27.0	27.0	27.0	27.0	27.0	27.0	27.0	27.0	27.0

C Class

21.0	22.5	28.9	34.2	30.3	23.1	22.4	19.0	18.6	14.0
18.0	17.9	18.0	18.0	18.0	18.0	18.0	18.0	18.0	18.0

D Class

14.7	14.3	16.3	22.8	27.8	24.2	18.1	17.0	15.2	13.0
15.0	15.0	14.9	15.0	15.0	15.0	15.0	15.0	15.0	15.0

ESF

87.2	88.2	89.5	86.1	86.7	87.1	87.7	83.0	90.0	88.9
90.5	89.0	89.0	89.0	89.0	89.0	89.0	89.0	89.0	89.0

III. Population

Total agency force (excluding retirees)

6587	6021	6269	6178	5968	5829	5929	5470	5469	5267
5650	5796	5967	6158	6371	6605	6860	7136	7433	7752

IV. Productivity, 1962–1981 (per capita production credits)

A Class

1157	1849	1922	1998	1870	1687	1704	2025	2575	2814
2704	2812	2925	3042	3163	3290	3421	3558	3701	3849

B Class

2687	3843	4709	4935	4995	5082	4949	5284	5824	6173
6008	6248	6498	6758	7029	7310	7602	7906	8222	8551

YEARS

1962	1963	1964	1965	1966	1967	1968	1969	1970	1971
1972	1973	1974	1975	1976	1977	1978	1979	1980	1981

C Class

3106	3685	4963	5493	5501	5616	5576	5903	6231	6888
6609	6873	7148	7434	7732	8041	8362	8697	9045	9407

D Class

3146	4308	4755	5607	5878	5720	6064	6206	6659	6914
7211	7499	7799	8111	8436	8773	9124	9489	9869	10264

ESF

3764	4308	4816	5372	6023	6305	6727	7956	8319	8820
8998	9358	9732	10122	10526	10947	11385	11841	12314	12807

V. Total Production Credits, Agency Expenses (thousands of dollars)

Total production credits

24176	26608	29774	32196	33569	33368	34578	37180	39565	41390
43078	45640	48376	51434	54849	58652	62874	67547	72706	78392

Percent yearly increase

5.6	10.1	11.9	8.1	4.3	−.6	3.6	7.5	6.4	4.6
4.1	5.9	6.0	6.3	6.6	6.9	7.2	7.4	7.6	7.8

Total agency department expenses

33550	36556	38731	43363	45523	47033	51987	60325	65356	70758
74288	79988	85611	91911	98717	106027	114112	123066	133153	144192

VI. Individual Life—Net Income from Operations

Many changes, including adding variable life in 1974 and projecting its market share to 19.8 percent of total production credits by 1981 (while individual life fell from 79 percent to 69 percent), produced the following income statement. (In particular, reduced growth cut the losses incurred from the initial costs of obtaining new policies.)

Net Income from Operations (millions of dollars)

					20.6	16.6	13.0	9.9	12.6
24.5	25.7	33.5	40.3	42.9	52.0	63.6	74.3	81.8	88.6

SOURCE: Reproduced with permission of The Equitable Life Assurance Society of the United States.

passengers by air" and "to provide for the distribution of goods by air." Therefore, the firm should be a *developer* of air transport with "control over the present and future supply of the major components of the total travel package." Hence, involvement in hotels, travel agencies, a helicopter company, and an air radio business followed.

The objectives were fourfold:

1. Twelve percent return on mean net assets.
2. Pay and productivity at best European levels.
3. High traffic growth and good market shares.
4. Acceptable noise levels.

These objectives were translated into quantified five year plans. For example, "A Distribution of Seat Miles by Section Length and Aircraft Size for 1988" facilitated the five year projection of aircraft and capacity, showing an increase in number from 214 in 1973 to 221 in 1978, with five Concordes and 60 percent of the capacity in Boeing 747's or larger! Employment was to rise from 52,900 to 54,800 but productivity was to jump 52 percent. Traffic was expected to rise 11 percent per year to generate earnings of £99.4 million or 12.5 percent on mean net assets.

NEW APPROACHES

In the past three or four years, several new approaches have evolved for the writing of objectives and the selection of appropriate strategies. Four in particular are (1) development of strategy alternatives, (2) resource allocation through portfolio management, (3) establishment of planning parameters, and (4) increasing use of contingency analyses.

strategy alternatives

Pinpointing strategy implications is facilitated by a rigorous requirement of viable "strategy alternatives." For example, General Electric's planning cycle starts early in the year and proceeds as follows:

1. The four-member Corporate Executive Office (CEO) reassesses the corporate mission, objectives, goals, and major policies in the light of forecast key environmental trends, and sets explicit corporate objectives and strategy

for the year. These are given to the 43 Strategic Business Units[11] (self-contained businesses which may be one of the 170 departments, one of 50 divisions, or one of 10 groups) together with the implications of the corporate strategy for the SBU spelled out in "preliminary planning guidelines," which might request that certain issues be explored or studies made and that alternate plans be prepared at accelerating or decelerating growth rates, and might even nominate one or more strategy alternatives to be developed by the SBU.

2. Meanwhile, each SBU is doing "bottom-up" strategic planning and evaluating proposals against its five-year market forecast (prepared against the backdrop of the corporate long-range environmental forecast as a base). After debate and review sessions with the Corporate Executive Office Staff (responsible for corporate plans), the SBUs recommend a strategy and one or more viable strategy alternatives complete with prices, payoffs, and required investments for alternative rates of growth and courses of action. Each alternative must be one the SBU can live with, should it be selected by the CEO.

3. The Corporate Executive Office then reviews all the SBU alternatives, decides on the optimum resource allocation, and transmits the final planning parameters and SBU strategy chosen.

4. On this basis, the SBU develops strategic plans and operating plans and budgets.

5. A final Corporate Executive Office planning review meeting concerns itself with "how to invest in these plans so as to optimize the attainment of the corporate objectives" set at the beginning of the year. To quote John B. McKitterick, vice president—Planning Development:

> We have sufficient good plans in hand to reach those objectives by several alternate paths which vary in risk and cost to implement. Factoring in the short range outlook, each plan is evaluated against several alternative possible economies, and then ranked in terms of its contribution to corporate long range and short term earnings.[12]

[11] A more complete description of the SBUs and their role in GE is given in Chapter 5.

[12] J. B. McKitterick, "Resource Allocation at the General Electric Company," speech given at the Conference on Economics, Crotonville, New York, November 22, 1971, p. 7.

6. Once the mix of plans is approved by the Corporate Executive Office, the SBUs prepare final operating budgets, cash budgets, and main appropriation proposals.

The process of hammering out the proper mix of alternatives through the interface of "top-down" and "bottom-up" planning takes months of negotiation. As Mr. McKitterick explained while the process was still being developed,

> For example, seeing threatening market trends, the corporation may want to explore the profit profile of a fast retreat. The SBU may want to meet the same threat head-on with a new plant, and after substantial outlays, achieve sizeable profits in later years.
>
> In practice, getting good final planning guidelines for each SBU has proven to be one of the most difficult and at the same time crucial requirements of the overall planning system. After all, the SBU management would like to have the advantage of being part of the General Electric Company, but none of the disadvantages. For the most part, everyone wants to grow, no one wants to "harvest." Everyone likes to procrastinate, few like to face up to implacable problems. Everyone likes to define an easy objective, no one likes to be measured against a tough one.[13]

Unfortunately, in most companies the requirement of viable strategy alternatives is given only lip service. It is much easier to go through the motions of proposing alternatives while actually designing the planning document so that only one choice has any real merit. Many divisional managers prefer to "sell their own pet plan upward" by giving their bosses no options.

resource allocation

The problem of allocating scarce resources—be they people or physical, financial, or intangible assets—has received increasing attention over the past five years.[14] Many companies are following General Electric's lead in utilizing "portfolio management," which means weighing the mix of strategies at agreed-upon risk levels for the appropriate business. In a diversified company, portfolio management means balancing the mix of businesses to fully utilize the corporate resources and take into account both the interaction between businesses and the differ-

---

[13] McKitterick, op. cit., p. 6.

[14] For an illuminating description of the financial resource allocation process at various middle- and top-management levels of a large, multiproduct company, see Joseph L. Bower, *Managing the Resource Allocation Process* (Cambridge, Mass.: Harvard Business School, 1970).

figure one

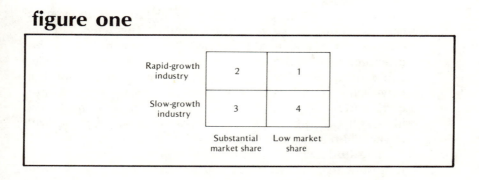

ing needs and risks of each. For an example in terms of financial resources only, we can categorize a business in the following market growth, market share matrix. (See Figure 1.)

Each square signifies differing cash needs and flows. Businesses in square 1 (low market share of a rapid-growth industry) require steady cash infusions to increase market share.[15] If and when it becomes a leader, the business moves to square 2 (substantial market share in a rapid-growth industry), and cash needs decline. Eventually, such a business becomes self-supporting, a leader, and generates excess cash for other businesses. Finally, as the product life cycle takes its toll, the mature business drifts into square 3 (substantial market share in a slow-growing industry) and becomes a cash generator for other businesses; hence the nickname "cash cow." As for square 4 (low market share in a slow-growth industry), this represents the "dying dogs" since improving market share in slow-growth, mature markets is usually prohibitively expensive. Such businesses are ripe for sale.

Classifying the financial portfolio helps ensure that a corporation will continue to develop cash generators (square 3); in

---

[15] Increased market share is usually needed in order to obtain the economies associated with larger volume (especially in high-fixed-cost industries that are volume sensitive). For many industries—such as automobiles or electrical equipment—the correlation between market share and ROI is direct (see "The Impact of Strategic Planning on Profit Performance" in *Harvard Business Review 52*, no. 2 (March–April 1974): 137–145, for a report on the PIMS study of the relationships of market share, product quality, investment intensity, and company factors to ROI). The predictable reduction in cost associated with increased volume is vividly demonstrated in The Boston Consulting Group, *Perspectives on Experience* (Boston, 1972), chap. 1.

fact, every growing business should be regarded as an eventual cash generator. Otherwise, it is a liability. This need, plus the shortage of available outside cash for many industries, has prompted increased pressure on operating managers to predict and control cash flows carefully. Financial resource allocation may well respond more to projections of cash than to forecasts of ROI. More companies may reject or defer projects with high ROI but substantial cash needs in favor of those with lower ROI but also reduced cash flows.

Since 1971 General Electric has used portfolio matrix analysis to ensure that resources are put behind products or services that (a) either already have or have the potential for high market share and profitable fast growth, or (b) contribute to GE's goal of building worldwide strengths in "businesses of the future," or (c) can yield very high short-term earnings or cash returns. The objective is to rank each SBU business as "green" (invest/grow—worldwide building on strength, with contained risk); "yellow" (selectivity—not requiring cash resources, with a deteriorating position or a plateaued business), or "red" (harvest/divest—high risk with a questionable future, or a special situation, or a "dog"). The first step for such a ranking is to evaluate on *one page* for each SBU area both industry attractiveness and business strengths in terms of market size and growth (differentiating between volume and price effects), competition, profitability ("contribution"), technical, and other. The evaluations for each of the 43 SBU's are plotted on a "Business Screen" as follows:

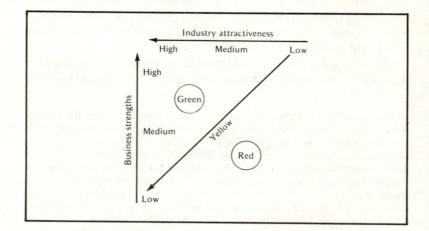

Clearly, green is in the high-high end, red in the low-low, and yellow in the middle.

Such a matrix leads first to the necessary dialogue between corporate planning and the SBU area and then to "priority strategic decisions"—what has to be done and in what order. Selected SBU plans (the key 20 out of 43 in 1974) are checked in depth against past experience and the Business Screen with respect to proposed activities in price, market, share, and cost to test the validity of the assumptions and recommendations. The mix of projected earnings from each business needed to reach a corporate target is shown on a "Quality of Earnings" matrix that ranks the estimates from hard to soft. Given these analyses, the chief executive officer can judge the acceptability of a SBU plan and thus confirm corporate level resource allocation decisions. This supports the management "value added" concept in a diverse enterprise.

planning parameters

Obtaining a *consistent hierarchy* of plans at a level of risk acceptable to top management poses severe implementation problems. One solution (adopted by General Electric, among others) is to have each level of the company—be it executive office, group, the new Strategic Business Unit, division, department, or section—set the planning guidelines or *parameters* for the level below. These guidelines might be the overall strategy and earnings target or might include specific objectives or key policies or even vital decisions that the higher executives did not want to leave to the discretion of their subordinates. Within these prescribed parameters, however, the manager is free to act. Properly implemented, this is freedom within clearly structured limits.

contingency analysis

An increasing number of companies stress "what if" contingency analysis to see (1) what it would cost and (2) what the management should do if the strategy goes wrong (contingency plans). First, the critical assumptions in the strategy should be identified and evaluated by the degree of confidence in and control over the assumption. Given the identified and ranked assumptions, one can pose the question, What if they were the opposite, or something different? The impact on planned results of the "what if" analysis (deviations from plan) helps determine whether to change objectives, strategy, or both.

Trigger points, or sensitive indicators, must be established to initiate the contingency plans if the "what if's" become reality. Updated "what if's" and contingency plans may provide earlier and more appropriate responses than ad hoc decisions.

recycling the planning output

Despite much preaching about the absolute necessity of having the planning cycle a *closed loop,* only a few firms have instituted *formal* recycling schedules to ensure that all divisional and departmental strategies and plans are (1) consistent vertically and horizontally and (2) constantly updated with *feedback* from the control system. Introducing a recycling program with specified dates for reviewing the planning outputs from other related areas is no more difficult than instituting formal planning, but the results can be most synergistic.

At a minimum, the process forces periodic review of one's own prose. The imaginative manager will find that even the most carefully worded objectives and policies can often be improved by adding quantitative evaluation criteria. For example, "excellence in product design" could be evaluated on cumulative five-year sales (assuming a five-year economic product life cycle), while "excellence in product quality" could be measured by (1) in-plant rejection rate (during final inspection) per unit sold, (2) customer complaints per unit sold, and (3) warranty service rate per unit sold. An instrument company has even devised a yardstick for "excellence in human resources." It is the ratio of value added (difference between dollar shipments and material costs) to employee compensation.[16]

SUMMARY

The techniques just discussed, as well as those being worked out in current practice, are designed to (1) make objectives, policies and plans more specific, quantified, and consistent; (2) link strategy with a rapidly changing environment; (3) en-

---

[16] "The Status of Long Range Planning," *The Conference Board Record 3,* no. 9 (September 1966): 9.

sure that all the viable strategy alternatives and their implications have been considered; (4) obtain needed input at the right time from all levels of management. This last objective is often instituted by means of a formal planning system, the subject of the next chapter.

four

FORMAL PLANNING SYSTEMS

Winston Churchill once said, "Planning is deciding to put one foot in front of the other." Certainly, most planning consists of making immediate, tangible action decisions and is seldom dignified by the word *planning*.

On the other hand, some projects clearly have to be planned in advance because of the lead time involved. For example, an electric utility that must by law supply the needs of all customers has to plan about four years in advance where to build the next substation, how large it should be, and so on. Almost as well known is the four- to five-year product planning cycle in the automobile industry. The lead times for market research, advanced styling explorations, and advanced engineering can take one and one-half years before the program is even approved. Another couple of years are taken by styling, engineering, tooling, and testing before production ("Job 1") starts—some three months in advance of dealer sales.[1]

In a sense, every manager is a planner, since almost every organization has both *goals* (either implicit or explicit) and limited *resources*. Long range planning means making explicit the implications for the future of today's resource allocation decisions. It does not mean making decisions in the future—attractive though the idea may be. After all, what we do today sets the framework for what we can do tomorrow.

The planning challenge of the 1970s was heralded by Mr. Cordiner of General Electric when he told the Economic Club of New York in March, 1966:

[1] For a description of this process together with the overall long-range planning cycle at Ford, see George A. Steiner, ed., *Managerial Long Range Planning* (New York: McGraw-Hill, 1963), pp. 232–234. Planners would argue that cycle times will get longer, not because of styling but for engineering and manufacturing to meet new federal safety, damageability, and emissions requirements.

The prime requisite of management is vision. The hallmark of wisdom is the ability to foresee with at least some clarity and confidence the needs of tomorrow and beyond tomorrow. If we are to achieve in fact a glorious economic future, our leaders in business must free themselves of this year's plans and programs and look at least 10 years ahead. The mounting problems and opportunities are making even a decade a short space of time for planning. More and more we should be planning fifteen or twenty years ahead—an entire business generation.[2]

Formalized long range planning first emerged during the late 1950s after the spate of policy manual writing initiated by Mr. Cordiner's publication of General Electric's objectives. "Formal" planning means "a planning effort to which various parts of the organization contribute through a system of formal procedures on a regular basis."[3]

INITIAL ATTEMPTS AT FORMAL PLANNING

The impetus behind most of the early formal plans may be viewed as either (1) the need for *coordinated* financial budgeting in capital intensive industries or (2) the desire for diversification and acquisition planning. A continuing formal planning study conducted at the Harvard Business School classified such companies as American Airlines, Caterpillar, and J. C. Penney in the first group; they were operating in relatively structured environments with homogeneous product lines and typically centralized management concerned with resource *availability*. On the other hand, the second group comprised such firms as Cities Service, Coca-Cola, General Mills, Johnson & Johnson, and Raytheon, with a multiplicity of products, a decentralized organizational structure, and a management interested in resource *allocation* through diversification.

The distinction between resource availability and resource allocation is important. Planning in response to questions of resource availability tends to be highly quantitative, rather than strategic, and to be initiated at the top; often—as with American Airlines' initial attempts in 1961—the aim is to coordinate departmental functional planning. The planners involved tend

---

[2] David W. Ewing, *Long Range Planning for Management* (New York: Harper & Row, 1958), p. 7.
[3] Richard F. Vancil et al., *Formal Planning Systems—1969* (Boston: Harvard Business School, 1969), p. 15.

to enjoy high status due to this close working relationship with the chief executive.

Resource allocation planning—such as was started at General Mills in the mid-1950s or at Raytheon in 1963—is strictly a bottom-up financial approach, sometimes beginning with the budget and without benefit of any corporate goals or divisional charters or objectives. Since the initial purpose was to identify growth opportunities, the plans were not used for management evaluation purposes. Some companies, such as Singer, were so anxious for divisional and departmental managers to be imaginative that diversification plans and even acquisitions of questionable long-term benefit were approved. The corporate planners performed advisory and coordination functions.

Despite such differences as type of company, product line, or planning objectives, the initial stages of formal planning for all companies studied had some significant similarities:

1. Planning was financially oriented, with the initial plans composed primarily of past trend extrapolation.
2. Planning was deliberately linked neither to the management evaluation process nor to the budget and control system in order not to stifle creativity or delay the start-up. (Those who started by coordinating the plan with the budget stopped after the first year.)
3. Planning was unrelated to any explicit objectives or strategies. In fact, *none* of the ten large companies studied had written goals or strategies.

As the report points out,

> Initiation of a planning system without explicit goals or strategy is contrary to the academic concept of a plan as the synthesis of a coordinated action program directing the entire organization towards established goals and objectives. The fact that goals may follow rather than precede formal planning suggests that the initial planning efforts serve to provide the information base necessary to facilitate top management thinking along these lines.[4]

Such explicit strategic thinking at the top was quick to come in multiproduct companies after formal planning was adopted. Organizations like General Mills found that bottom-up planning led to a corporate–divisional dialogue, with the result that explicit corporate objectives and strategies were set. However,

---

[4] Vancil et al., op. cit., p. 23.

single-product companies saw little need for such explicit goals to facilitate functional, departmental financial planning.

Parallel with the shift to strategic planning, multiproduct companies also were quick to link plans with budget. The start was reconciling the budget with only the first year of the plan, but soon each budget was formulated in the light of prior plans, and any deviations had to be justified.

EMERGING ALTERNATE APPROACHES

During the late 1960s several clear approaches to planning emerged. First, there were many companies for which planning was strictly financial forecasting and budgeting. The format and emphasis varied—pro forma income statements, pro forma balance sheets, cash flow projections, capital expenditure forecasts—depending partly on the type of business and product involved. An example of what were often lengthy and complex forms is shown in Exhibit 1; each Motorola division manager had 20 such pages to fill in.

Often the paper work disguised the fact that financial planning was predominant. The sheets to be filled in might well include complex market forecasts, competitive analyses, or detailed plans for all functional areas; only the experienced divisional manager knew "what the head office was really interested in."

The second type of planning resembled the first except that the nonfinancial sections were considered the most important; the financial projections were merely interpreting and coordinating the actual planning done elsewhere. An example of such planning is Motorola in the mid-1960s; the highly structured format was shown in Exhibit 3 of Chapter 3. It is interesting to note how much detail and specific planning top management expected.

The third type was an offshoot of the first two and might loosely be called programed project planning. It consisted of narrowly focused, in-depth studies of particular projects—such as a new-product introduction, a new factory going on stream, or the completion of a weapons system. Out of the increasing number of systems contracts for the Department of Defense emerged integrating tools to minimize time and/or cost called Critical Part Method (CPM) and Program Evaluation Review Technique (PERT).

exhibit one

MOTOROLA, BUSINESS MACHINES DIVISION, FIVE-YEAR FORECAST, 1967–1971

Form (D)

TOTAL DIVISION P&L STATEMENT

1961	1966 CURRENT FORECAST AS OF	$ IN 000's	% CHANGE 1961 1966	% CHANGE 1966 1971	1967	1971
		Sales Before Disc/Allow				
		Disc/Allow				
		Division Correction Factor				
		Net Sales (see Note 1)				
		Mfgr. Cost—Material				
		Std. Direct Labor				
		Overhead				
		Dies (if significant)				
		TOTAL MFGR. COST				
		Engineering				
		Mktg. & Selling				
		Division G&A				
		Corp. G&A/Corp. Acctg. Serv.				
		PS/SCRP				
		Operating Income				
		Royalty Income/(Expense)				
		Other Income/(Expense)				
		Interest (Expense)/Income				
		Division Correction Factor				
		Net Income				

Notes:
(1) Net Sales—Internal
            —External
(2) Consolidated Int'l
      Oper. Included Above:
      Net Sales
      Net Income
(3) Depreciation—
      Straight Line
      Below Line

Form (I)

1961	1966 CURRENT FORECAST AS OF	$ IN 000's	% CHANGE 1961 1966	% CHANGE 1966 1971	1967	1971
		AVERAGE INVESTMENT				
		Cash (25% of Ave. Mo. Sales)				
		Receivables (w/# Wks. Supply)				
		Less Allow. for Uncollected A/C's				
		Inv./Costs Recov. (w/# Wks. Supply)				
		Prod. Mat'l				
		Work in Process				
		Finished Goods				
		Costs Recov.				
		Other				
		TOTAL INV./COSTS REC.				
		Fixed Assets (From Form J)				
		L/H Improv., Dies—Net				
		Corporate Alloc.				
		Other Assets				
		TOTAL AVERAGE INVEST-MENT (2)				
		INVESTMENT TURNOVERS (w/% of Total Investment)				
		Receivables—Net				
		Inventories/Cost Recov.				
		Fixed Assets				
		Cash and All Other Assets				
		TOTAL AVERAGE IN-VESTMENT				
		ROI COMPUTATION				
		Net Sales				
		Net Income After Interest				
		Reversal of Interest				
		Net Income Before Interest (4)				
		% of Net Income Before Interest to Sales (1)				
		TOTAL AVERAGE IN-VESTMENT (2)				
		Net sls ÷ Total Ave. Inv. (turnover) (3)				
		ROI = (1) × (3)				
		= (4) ÷ (2)				
		These results must be equal.				

The fourth type of planning focused on either (1) the skills or strengths of the company or division or (2) its weaknesses or scarce resources. The latter is easier to do. For example, capital intensive industries with long lead times, such as airframe or oil companies, have long emphasized facilities planning. The philosophy is that fixed asset investments made today set the framework for the company of the future. Likewise, high-technology companies focus on the projected R&D expenses; clearly, how these dollars are spent will set the direction for the future. Indeed, Stanford Research Institute places great emphasis on the R&D plan. Other companies, especially in the life insurance industry, often start with projections of manpower skill requirements; this has been partly responsible for the increased popularity of manpower data banks in large firms.

Planning around skills is much more difficult, since not only must the skills first be identified and agreed upon, but the formal system itself must be tailor-made. No longer can one borrow the format used by the industry, the trade association, or a competitor. The planning system must be totally integrated, from corporate concept through objectives through strategy, plans, and budgets.

Whatever system is used, effective planning is a continuous process. It is not a "sometime" thing—that easily delegated, part-time management activity. Rather, managers must be continuously sensitive to the long-run implications of any change, be it in the environment, corporate skills, business strategy, or actions. Such sensitivity can be fostered by using the business plan as the appropriate framework against which change can be measured and the value of alternative actions appraised. To quote the Westinghouse *Guide to Business Planning,*

> Effective planning enhances management's response to change. Far from committing management to a fixed course of action, a good plan evaluates many alternatives and provides a range of choices for responding to changing conditions. Furthermore, the planning activity in itself focuses management's attention on potential opportunities and on potential threats before they occur, thus providing valuable lead time for taking appropriate action.[5]

FORMAL PLANNING FRAMEWORKS

Setting a formal framework helps ensure that the planning is consistent and continuous. The General Electric schematic pro-

[5] Westinghouse Electric Corp., *Guide to Business Planning,* p. 7.

figure one

ENVIRONMENTAL ANALYSIS			
ENVIRONMENT SECTORS	**TECHNICAL DIMENSION**	**POLITICAL DIMENSION**	**ECONOMIC DIMENSION**
Society			
Markets			
Customers			
Industry			
Suppliers			
Government			

gram starts with a matrix to be filled out on environmental analysis, as in Figure 1.[6]

General Electric defines strategic planning as "that activity which specifies for a business a course of action that is designed to achieve desired long term objectives in the light of all major external and internal factors, present and future." The company defines the 11 major elements of a strategic plan proposed by a Strategic Business Unit (SBU) as follows:

1. The statement of the SBU's *Mission*—what it is, why it exists, and the unique contribution it can make to the Company.
2. The *Key Environmental Assumptions*—these summarize the nature of the external environment in which the business will be working, and the opportunities and threats which the SBU sees in the environment.
3. *Key Competitor Assumptions*—including estimates of the strengths and limitations of competitors and judgments of their probable plans.

[6] "Strategic Planning: Some Help for the Businessman," *Air Conditioning, Heating and Refrigeration News 126*, no. 9, (June 26, 1972): 12. Copyright 1972.

4. A list of *Constraints*—the forces either from inside or outside the Company that may limit the SBU's choice of actions.
5. *Objectives*—the desired future position or destination the SBU wants to attain.
6. The *Goals*—the specific time-based points of measurement that the SBU intends to meet in the pursuit of its objectives.
7. The *Strategy*—the course of action the SBU intends to follow to achieve its objectives, while meeting goals along the way.
8. *Programs*—development, investment, or other programs that are critical to the pursuit of the SBU's strategy.
9. The required *Resources* and sources—the things it takes to do the job, and where they are to be obtained.
10. *Contingencies* and the associated "what if" contingency plans, which recognize that things might go wrong along the way and ask what it might cost if they do, and what the SBU plans to do if they do go wrong.
11. The last element of a strategic plan is the SBU *Long-Range Forecast*. This is the expression in financial terms of the first ten elements of the strategic plan.[7] Programmed, the elements appear as in Figure 2.[8]

an example of formal planning

Even without substantive content examples, the formal planning system paper work may indicate much about a company's approach to strategy. The Westinghouse system used through 1972 is a good example of the formal planning approaches instituted by many large companies during the 1960s.

the business strategy narrative

In theory, at least, the Westinghouse divisional profit plan is a communication device that summarizes, in quantitative form, the entire planning process for communication both within the division and to top management. For this to happen, the key elements of the strategy must be outlined in ten double-spaced pages or less in the Business Strategy Narratives. The financial implications of at least 50 percent of the division's planned Strategic Managed Costs[9] are to be summarized on

[7] "GE's Evolving Management System," January 18, 1972, pp. 17–18. (Internal presentation, quoted with permission of General Electric Co.)
[8] *Air Conditioning, Heating and Refrigeration News,* op. cit., p. 12.
[9] Strategic Managed Costs are the semifixed expenditures that are within the division management's discretion for the long run, not the year at hand.

figure two

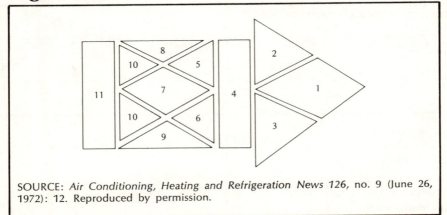

SOURCE: *Air Conditioning, Heating and Refrigeration News* 126, no. 9 (June 26, 1972): 12. Reproduced by permission.

the Strategic Program Analysis forms. (See Exhibit 2.) The text is supposed to refer to the summarized key programs "that have a major impact on profitability and make an important contribution to future performance." The priorities of action are to be indicated, together "with an indication of *which* strategic programs will have *what* influences on the attainment of current objectives."

Although "considerable room is allowed for discretion and flexibility in reporting," the narrative outline is supposed to cover seven points. They are

1. *A brief review of prior plans* (as background for the current plan). Included should be a brief paragraph describing significant changes between, for example, 1971 plans for 1973 and the current (1972) objectives for 1973.
2. *An assessment of the market* and key environmental factors. This section should discuss the market environment, short and long range, including comments on market growth, market penetration, and product prices.
3. *A statement of the business strategy* in view of the market situation and other key environmental factors.
4. *A description of the strategic programs* to accomplish the strategy.
5. *Identification of the sensitive indicators* that should provide early warning signs triggering the reduced operating

exhibit two

managed costs plan as shown in the manpower planning and support data sections (to be discussed).

6. *The expected contribution of strategic programs* for achieving long-range objectives. Here the steps currently in progress (or to be taken) to meet long-range goals should be described.

7. *An outline of any major projects or facilities investments* needed to implement the plan.

Even to a disinterested outsider, the task of compressing all seven points into ten pages seems Herculean indeed! Still, Mr. Churchill once asked for the plans for the naval defense of Great Britain to be summarized in one page.

the market planning summary

Called Form 1 (see Exhibit 3), this is the basic summary of both cyclical forecasts and Westinghouse's sales objectives; it underlies the financial objectives shown in other portions of the formal or profit plan. Shown is five years' history, the current year objective and forecast, the forecast for next year (1975), and plans for the following three years (1976–1978). The latter may be developed on a trend or a cyclical basis as the division management wishes.

the profit pattern analysis

Called Form 2 (see Exhibit 4), this shows the changes from the original forecast that led to the formal objective for next year. This form is really a translation of the business strategy narrative and subsidiary plans into a variable (or direct product cost) budget for subsequent comparison with actual results (a "Statement 6," in Westinghouse terminology).[10]

the investment strategy narrative

Each division's investment plans are to be summarized in three double-spaced pages or less and the numbers entered on the form shown in Exhibit 5. The end result—and key number— is the cash flow.

[10] For a quantitative understanding of the Westinghouse variable budgeting system, see David C. D. Rogers, *The Manager's Guide to Budgeting and Control Systems* (Ann Arbor, Mich.: The Landis Press, 1974).

exhibit three

A MARKET PLANNING SUMMARY

FORM 1

PRODUCT LINES

DIVISION

LINE NO.	MARKET & WESTINGHOUSE VOLUME ARE ☐ ORDERS ☐ SALES	1969	HISTORY 1970	1971	1972	1973	1974 OBJECTIVE	1974 FORECAST	1975 FORECAST	PLANS 1976	1977	1978
	DOMESTIC MARKETING MARKETS											
1A	CUSTOMER (INCL. IMPORTS)											
1B	INTERUNIT											
1C	TOTAL											
	WESTINGHOUSE VOLUME											
2A	CUSTOMER											
2B	INTERUNIT											
2C	OTHER											
2D	TOTAL											
	PENETRATION – %											
3A	CUSTOMER											
3B	INTERUNIT											
3C	TOTAL											
	NON-DOMESTIC MARKETING MARKETS											
4A	EXPORTS FROM U.S. (OTHER THAN CANADIAN)											
4B	EXPORTS TO CANADA (INCL. (W) CANADA)											
4C	OTHER AVAILABLE NON-DOMESTIC MARKETS											
4D	TOTAL AVAILABLE NON-DOMESTIC MARKETS											
	WESTINGHOUSE VOLUME											
5A	EXPORTS FROM U.S. (OTHER THAN CANADIAN)											
5B	EXPORTS TO CANADA (INCL. (W) CANADA)											
5C	OTHER NON-DOMESTIC VOLUME											
5D	TOTAL AVAILABLE NON-DOMESTIC VOLUME											
	PENETRATION – %											
6A	EXPORTS FROM U.S. (OTHER THAN CANADIAN)											
6B	EXPORTS TO CANADA (INCL. (W) CANADA)											
6C	OTHER AVAILABLE NON-DOMESTIC MARKETS											
6D	TOTAL AVAIL. NON-DOMESTIC PENETRATION–%											
	PRICE REALIZATION (O.E. = 100.)											
7A	ORDERS – TOTAL											
7B	SALES – TOTAL											
7C	EXPORT (MEMO) SALES ☐ ORDERS ☐											
	ANNUAL TREND GROWTH RATE – %	-73	74-79									
8A	DOMESTIC MARKET (LINE 1A)	%	%									
8B	WESTINGHOUSE SALES – DOM MKT. (LINE 2A)	%	%									
10	TOTAL WESTINGHOUSE ORDERS											
11	TOTAL WESTINGHOUSE SALES											
12	FOREIGN LICENSING INCOME – GROSS											

MEMO DATA
ADDITION TO PROD. LINE (AFTER 74)
9A MARKET
9B WESTINGHOUSE VOLUME
9C PENETRATION – %

	HISTORY		FORECAST	
	1972	1973	1974	1975

COMPETITION – COMPANIES & %	HISTORY		FORECAST	
	1971	1973	1974	1975

PRODUCT NAMES & WESTINGHOUSE CODE NUMBERS FOR DATA ON THIS FORM

SOURCE OF MARKET DATA

SOURCE: Reproduced by permission of Westinghouse Electric Corp.

exhibit four

THE PROFIT PATTERN ANALYSIS

DIVISION _____   FORM 2   DATE _____

ST. 6 LINE NO.	DESCRIPTION	(A) 1974 FORECAST	(B) PHYSICAL VOLUME	(C) PRICE CHANGES	(D) MIX CHANGES	(E) GENERAL PAYROLL	(F) OTHER PAYROLL	(G) MATERIAL PRICE	(H) POLICY CHANGES	(I)	(J)	(K) ACCTG. CHANGES	(L) PLANNED COST IMP.	(M) 1975 FORECAST	ST. 6 LINE NO.
5	SALES														5
6	TOTAL OTHER INCOME														6
7	TRANSPORTATION COST														7
8	COMPENSATION ON SALES & CASH DISCOUNT														8
9	OTHER SALES DEDUCTIONS														9
10	DIRECT COSTS - LABOR														10
11	- MATERIAL														11
12	- FACTORY EXPENSE														12
13	CUSTOMER ORDER DEVELOPMENT - SHOP														13
14	ENGINEERING CONTRACTS														14
15	PRODUCT WARRANTY														15
16	OTHER														16
17	DIRECT PRODUCT COSTS														17
18	MARGIN OVER DIRECT PRODUCT COSTS														18
19	MANUFACTURING														19
20	ENGINEERING														20
21	MARKETING														21
22	ADMINISTRATIVE & GENERAL														22
23	OTHER														23
24	TOTAL OPERATING MANAGED COSTS														24
26	DEPRECIATION & LEASE COSTS														26
27	INS. & TAXES — HOL. & VACATIONS														27
28	DIVISION COMMITTED COSTS														28
29	INVENTORY CHANGE EFFECT ON IBT														29
30	TOTAL OPER. COSTS DIV. CONTROLLED														30
31	INTEREST EXPENSE														31
32	GROUP AND COMPANY MANAGED COSTS														32
33	CORPORATE MANAGED COSTS														33
34	TOTAL OPERATING COSTS														34
35	**MARGIN OVER OPERATING COSTS**														**35**
36	MANUFACTURING														36
37	ENGINEERING														37
38	MARKETING														38
39	ADMINISTRATIVE & GENERAL														39
40	RESEARCH & DEVELOPMENT														40
41	OTHER														41
42	TOTAL STRATEGIC MANAGED COSTS														42
43	TOTAL COSTS														43
44	INCOME BEFORE TAXES														44
45	INCOME TAXES														45
46	INVESTMENT & DISC TAX CREDITS														46
47	INCOME AFTER TAXES														47
48	INCOME AFTER TAXES - MINORITY INTEREST														48
49	INCOME AFTER TAXES - WESTINGHOUSE														49

* CONTRA IN COST AND EXPENSE. † LOSS ON LINES 44, 47, 48 & 49. ‡ UNFAVORABLE EFFECT ON INCOME LINE 29

exhibit five

INVESTMENT MANAGEMENT

YEAR-END BALANCES	1970 ACT.	1971 OBJ.	1971 FCST.	1972 PLANS OBJ.	1972 PLANS PRIOR	1973 PLAN	1976 PLAN
CASH-OPER. REQMT.							
CUSTOMER INVESTMENT							
NOTES & ACCTS. REC. — TRADE							
NET INVENTORIES							
PROG. & ADV. BILLING							
ALL OTHER CURRENT ASSETS							
TOTAL CUST. INVEST.							
LONG TERM INVESTMENT							
TOTAL PLANT & EQUIP. NET							
ALL OTHER ASSETS							
TOTAL LONG TERM INVEST.							
LIABILITIES							
ACCTS. PAYABLE TRADE							
SUBS BANK LOANS & OVERDRAFTS							
ALL OTHER LIAB. & MINOR. INT.							
TOTAL LIABILITIES							
CORPORATE INVESTMENT							
INTEREST EXPENSE (MEMO)	( )	( )	( )	( )	( )	( )	( )
SOURCE & USE OF FUNDS							1974
SOURCE:							-75
INCOME AFTER TAXES							-76
DEPRECIATION							
CUSTOMER INVESTMENT							
ACCTS. PAYABLE TRADE							
SUBS BANK LOANS & OVERDRAFTS							
OTHER							
TOTAL							
USE:							
OPERATING LOSS							
CUSTOMER INVESTMENT							
ACCTS. PAYABLE TRADE							
PLANT & EQUIP. ADDITIONS							
OTHER							
TOTAL							
NET CASH FLOW (TO CORP.)							
NET CASH FLOW (FROM CORP.)							

SOURCE: Reproduced by permission of Westinghouse Electric Corp.

More than ever, control of cash flow in Westinghouse is of the utmost importance due to the growth of both short and long term debt which has increased interest expense and lowered corporate profit. Therefore, the narrative should emphasize specific actions planned to improve cash flow and minimize both short and long term debt.[11]

Suggestions for minimizing current assets are included. For example, to reduce notes and accounts receivable it is suggested that a specific program be mounted, suspense items be kept at a minimum, terms of sales be "competitive but profitable," and nonstandard terms be eliminated. Under inventories, the *Profit Plan Book* states: "Explain the two or three major items and their dollar contribution to the planned change in the Inventory Investment from year end 1971 to year end 1972."

The suggestions end with a couple of comments about the net cash flow:

The narrative should discuss how the 1972 net cash flow objective will be met if economic conditions do not materialize as planned.
Include two or three major areas of sensitivity that could cause a detraction in meeting the 1972 Net Cash Flow objective.[12]

Omitted are any references to maximizing accounts payable and other non-interest-bearing current liabilities—consistent with taking discounts—that also reduce corporate investment.

supporting documents

The final three forms elaborate on the key documents already presented. The first is a Planned Cost & Expense Improvement Analysis (see Exhibit 6) showing the status and the income before tax (IBT) of all current and projected projects. (The results are summarized in Column L of the Profit Planning Analysis.) The second is the Manpower Planning Form. (See Exhibit 7.) In a supporting two and one-half pages, the division manager is supposed to answer:

1. What actions are you taking to fill requirements for any critical skills needs you anticipate?

[11] *Westinghouse Electric Corporation Profit Plan Book,* (Pittsburgh, Pa.) November 3, 1971.
[12] Ibid.

exhibit six

PLANNED COST AND EXPENSE IMPROVEMENT

_____ DIVISION

PROJECT STATUS & DESCRIPTION	19 FORECAST		FIRST FULL YEAR
	DOLLARS	% IBT EFFECT	TOTAL PROJECT EFFECT IN $
1. PROJECTS ALREADY IMPLEMENTED			
TOTAL			
2. PROJECTS NOW BEING IMPLEMENTED			
TOTAL			
3. PROJECTS DOCKETED			
TOTAL			
4. PROJECTS TO BE INITIATED			
TOTAL			
5. TOTAL IBT EFFECT (FORM 2, LINE 44, COLUMN L) (FORM 2B, LINE 43, COLUMN L)			
6. TOTAL IAT EFFECT (FORM 2, LINE 47, COLUMN L) (FORM 2B, LINE 46, COLUMN L)			

SOURCE: Reproduced by permission of Westinghouse Electric Corp.

exhibit seven

MANPOWER PLANNING FORM

_____ Division

		DEC. 19 ACTUAL	DEC. 19 FORECAST	DEC. 19 FORECAST
ENGINEERING	– SALARY			
	– FUNDED			
	– HOURLY			
MARKETING	– SALARY			
	– FUNDED			
	– HOURLY			
ADMINISTRATION	– SALARY			
	– FUNDED			
	– HOURLY			
FIELD SERVICES	– SALARY			
	– FUNDED			
	– HOURLY			
MANUFACTURING	– SALARY			
	– FUNDED			
	– HOURLY PRODUCTIVE			
	– HOURLY EXPENSE			
TOTAL SALARY				
	– FUNDED			
TOTAL HOURLY				

SOURCE: Reproduced by permission of Westinghouse Electric Corp.

2. What three significant personnel problem areas do you forsee during 1973, and what plans do you have for coping with them?

The resulting manpower estimates at 15 percent above and below the budget objective are crucial inputs for the next form.

The third supporting document, Operating Managed Costs Budget Adjustment (see Exhibit 8), is perhaps the most confusing part of the profit plan. Operating Managed Costs (OMC) are those incurred in "getting the product out the door," as distinct from the direct product costs (line 17 of Exhibit 4), which theoretically should vary directly with unit volume. OMC is a mixture of fixed and variable costs and as such should change at a lower rate or in steplike fashion with significant shifts in volume. In correlating changes from objective levels of OMC and unit volume, the Westinghouse corporate guideline is that the OMC should rise 2.5 percent for every 10 percent increase in sales and drop 5 percent for every 10 percent volume decrease; however, such a formula may not work for a particular division. In fact, the division should use a profit pattern simulation, step level budgeting, or regression analysis of past history to arrive at a useful OMC formula. To quote the *Profit Plan Book*, "the method chosen should be based on some sensitive indicator such as backlog, orders entered, or Net Allowed Hours (NAH) that provides early warning signs pointing to the need for adjustment."[13]

In 1973, Westinghouse instituted a new planning system and separated the annual profit plan from the strategic plan. The profit plan, due in the fourth quarter, focuses on next year and is highly financial in nature with sales, operations, income, etc. analyzed and projected (as shown in Exhibits 4, 6–8). The market is forecasted for five years on Form I (Exhibit 3).

The strategic plan, due in the spring, is longer range (minimum of five years, longer for certain businesses). It emphasizes the business review, the environment for growth, key strategic goals, strategies and programs, the financial implications, and contingency plans. The separation was made to insure that long range planning was not deemphasized due to short-term profit pressures, as happens in too many other companies.

---

[13] Ibid.

exhibit eight

OPERATING MANAGED COSTS BUDGET ADJUSTMENT

————————————————————— DIVISION

LINE NO.	DESCRIPTION	15% BELOW SALES FORECAST	19 FORECAST	15% ABOVE SALES FORECAST	STMT. 6 LINE NO.
1	SALES				5
2	DIRECT PRODUCT COSTS				17
3	MARGIN				18
4	MANUFACTURING				19
5	ENGINEERING				20
6	MARKETING				21
7	ADMINISTRATIVE & GENERAL				22
8	OTHER OPERATING MANAGED COSTS				23
9	TOTAL OPERATING MANAGED COSTS				24
10	OPERATING MANAGED COSTS AS % OF SALES (MEMO)				
11	ALL OTHER				
12	MARGIN OVER OPERATING COSTS				35
13	STRATEGIC MANAGED COSTS				42
14	INCOME BEFORE TAXES				44
15	INCOME TAXES AND TAX CREDIT				45 & 46
16	INCOME AFTER TAXES				47
17	INCOME AFTER TAXES - MIN. INT.				48
18	INCOME AFTER TAXES				49

METHOD USED TO DEVELOP OPERATING MANAGED COSTS:

CORPORATE GUIDELINE ☐

ANALYSIS OF COST BEHAVIOR ☐

OTHER_____ ☐
(DESCRIBE)

SOURCE: Reproduced by permission of Westinghouse Electric Corp.

THE FUTURE OF FORMAL PLANNING

To many observers, formal planning systems are in a state of limbo. Some feel that the payoff simply hasn't been apparent. They point out that most of the planning literature has been written by formal planning specialists, and the examples frequently cited—such as Lockheed Aircraft—are unfortunate at best. Too often managers do not see the formal system as a way of eliciting widespread commitment to planning. The plans may remain unused from one annual planning session to another or —as is even more common—managers perceive meeting the budget and short-term results as key to their success and deploy their time accordingly.

Still others point to the growing use of the computer as the facilitator of widespread and effective formal planning. They can point to the growth of data banks, the use of "sophisticated" tools such as decision trees,[14] and the over 200 companies that claim to do computer modeling.[15]

Unfortunately, most of the models are really just financial forecasting devices. Much discussion has centered on the models devised in the oil and utility and airline industries, where most of the transactions are on a price basis and there are heavy fixed costs and a high capital investment.[16] However, a financial planning model devised by Sun Oil required 1500 separate inputs, while one developed by Detroit Edison needed two months to prepare the input data for a single run.[17] Few top-line managers have the time, inclination, or requisite skills to assimilate and use such massive programs. Small wonder the Sun Oil program was no longer used after the company merged and the original developers left!

Strategic planning is conducted by general managers in an unstable, highly political environment. Line managers often are

[14] Rex V. Brown, "Do Managers Find Decision Theory Useful?" *Harvard Business Review 48,* no. 3 (May–June 1970): 78–89.

[15] G. W. Gershefski, "Corporate Models—The State of the Art," *Managerial Planning 18,* no. 3 (November–December 1969): 1–6.

[16] James B. Boulden and Elwood S. Buffa, "Corporate Models: On-line, Real-time Systems," *Harvard Business Review 48,* no. 4 (July–August 1970): 65–83.

[17] Descriptions of the models are found in G. W. Gershefski, "Building a Corporate Financial Model," *Harvard Business Review 47,* no. 4 (July–August 1969), and in D. C. Achtenberg and R. E. Landback, "A Computerized Financial Model for an Electric Utility," *Proceedings of IEEE Summer Power Meeting,* 1970.

not involved or even consulted in development of the computer program, do not understand its potential, and regard the results as an oversimplification of the real world.[18] For example, airline companies (especially British Airways) have developed highly sophisticated interactive models for passenger and fare forecasts, aircraft allocation and costing, sale and purchases of equipment, financial forecasts, schedule construction, and a host of tactical short-term planning programs. Notwithstanding, top management frequently overrules the planners' conclusions with respect to the acquisition and sale of aircraft and even the allocation of equipment to particular routes. Reasons given are "political problems" or "competitive equipment decisions" that are "too hard to input into the program."

The day when real-time models will be used by top management for strategic planning seems distant. First, there are the problems of developing models that are sufficiently complex to be realistic, yet not too time-consuming or involved as to frighten the nonspecialist manager. Industries, such as oil, in which most of the intra- and interindustry interfaces are on a commodity price basis, is a rational place to start, yet even in the oil industry many of the models are financial and are not utilized. The second problem is that most planning is really done by lower management, with top management approving or disapproving the one alternative presented. So-called bottom-up management is very characteristic of formal planning.

Some observers feel that formal planning systems will be more useful once (1) planning is connected to budgeting but not submerged and (2) managers are evaluated and compensated on strategic planning as well as on current operations. Much creative work needs to be done on compensation schemes before planning will become truly an integrated part of the manager's job. In the meantime, new and imaginative approaches to organizational structure are emerging as a tool for implementing strategy and fostering planning; this is the focus of the next chapter.

[18] For an interesting research-based discussion of the current plight of computer-based systems, see William K. Hall, "Strategic Planning Models: Are Top Managers Really Finding Them Useful?" *Journal of Business Policy 3*, no. 3 (Spring 1973).

five

CORPORATE STRATEGY AND ORGANIZATION STRUCTURE: THE SIAMESE TWINS

Most textbooks on strategy either avoid the knotty problem of formal organization or dive headlong into laborious descriptions of various organizational formats and their historical evolution.[1] These descriptions usually start with a discussion of purpose—"the central aim of organization is to divide and reunify work to accomplish the company's objectives in the market"—and then lapse into definitions and principles.[2] A typical list of the latter is the following, gleaned from a recent offering.[3]

PRINCIPLES OF ORGANIZATION
1. Establish clear objectives.
2. Assign each necessary function.
3. Avoid duplicate functions.
4. Limit the functions per individual.
5. Group related functions; separate unrelated functions.

[1] A concise approach of this sort may be found in J. Thomas Cannon, *Business Strategy and Policy* (New York: Harcourt Brace Jovanovich, 1968), pp. 303–343. A good description and critique of traditional organizational theory (with some well-known examples) are in Rocco Carzo, Jr., and John N. Yanouzas, *Formal Organization: A Systems Approach* (Homewood, Ill.: Irwin–Dorsey, 1967), pp. 23–102. The most thorough treatments are in Joseph A. Litterer, *Organizations: Structure and Behavior*, 2d ed. (New York: Wiley, 1969), a two-volume collection of readings, and Joseph A. Litterer, *The Analysis of Organization* (New York: Wiley, 1965). Examples of business practice during the heyday of formal organization theorizing are in K. K. White, *Understanding the Company Organization Chart* (New York: American Management Association, 1963). The best summary of formal and informal organization is in Edmund P. Learned and Audrey T. Sproat, *Organization Theory and Policy: Notes for Analysis* (Homewood, Ill.: Irwin, 1966).

[2] Cannon, op. cit., p. 308.

[3] Ibid., p. 312.

6. Use consistent patterns by level.
7. Define responsibilities clearly.
8. Match responsibility with authority.
9. Delegate decision making to the lowest level possible.
10. Clarify reporting relationships.
11. Avoid more than one boss per individual.
12. Avoid excessive levels.
13. Keep the organization simple.
14. Avoid excessive structural changes.

Designing a formal organization really means *splitting up* an agreed-upon strategy into an impersonal system of coordinated activities (or task assignments) that specifies who is to do what. The resulting structure, simple or complex, is determined basically by the needs of *division of labor* on the one hand and *coordination* on the other. In defining tasks, the general manager must (1) identify all key decisions or essential management activities (2) provide for these decisions and activities by splitting up or delegating authority and responsibility (while retaining ultimate accountability) into manageable units, and (3) coordinate and integrate the separated specialized efforts to ensure that they are consistent with corporate strategy and objectives. The process has been summed up as follows: "The division of labor is thus accompanied by the specialization of task and the distribution of authority, with the relative importance of tasks as defined by strategy marked by status.[4]

However, the coordination side of formal organization design is the most complicated. The naturally conflicting interests and viewpoints of individuals, departments, divisions, or functional areas must be compromised because, as stated in Chapter 1, what is best for the company as a whole is always suboptimal for any subunit. But the reintegration of divided specialized tasks can be a most creative process if the rivalry between competing units is kept constructive and focused on corporate strategy. Out of constructive disagreement can come a whole that is really greater than the sum of its parts. To quote Kenneth Andrews again,

The ability to handle the coordinating function in a way that brings about a new synthesis among competing interests, a synthesis in harmony with the special competence of the total or-

---

[4] Kenneth R. Andrews, *The Concept of Corporate Strategy* (Homewood, Ill.: Dow Jones–Irwin, 1971), p. 188.

ganization, is the administrator's most subtle and creative contribution to the successful functioning of an organization.[5]

Some formal organization—even the limited structuring and clarifying of informal activities prescribed for small and growing firms—can extend the ability to accomplish tasks from the individual to the group and help perpetuate the company. A general manager limits the scope and life of his organization by his own physical capacity unless he divides up the job and so provides bailiwicks for individual decision making and freedom of action.

The formal organization sets the framework within which the informal organization operates; however, to be effective the formal must be related to the informal and must not impede teamwork. The job of building an organization is never finished, and it is one that the general manager cannot delegate completely.

STRUCTURAL FORMS

The organization structure should be arranged by the dictates of strategy, not by the industry pattern, the historical custom of the company, the general manager's preferences, or the opinions of an outside "authority." Still, there are some general caveats and "typical" patterns. For example, the basis of dividing up tasks should be relatively consistent and understandable, encourage teamwork, allow for structural change, and be clearly related to corporate goals and strategy.

The increasing size and complexity of operations motivate managers to try new forms of organization. For example, the one-man retailer expands to a *functional organization* with sales and manufacturing separated, and later adds specialized staff activities (such as accounting or personnel). More growth may lead to a *geographic organization,* with separate line and some key staff activities in each area. Multinational companies often divisionalize geographically on the assumption that the key variables and problems are peculiar to each area. Larger companies usually install a corporate staff to handle financial, personnel, legal, research, or other functions that are not to be delegated to the geographic division.

Additional products or the acquisition of subsidiaries may lead to a *product organization,* with sales, manufacturing, usu-

[5] Ibid., p. 193.

ally engineering, and some staff functions delegated to product division managers. Increasing size and diversity brings the need for coordination, with resultant proliferation of corporate staffs. Corporate marketing is one of the first to appear.

If the number of product divisions increases so that there are too many to report to one chief executive, the *group organization* concept is substituted, whereby several divisions (sometimes with a semblance of synergy) report to a single group executive; there may be several of the latter. In addition, all staff services may report to one or more group executives in order to ease the burden on top management.

Sometimes functional or product organizations spawn a hybrid, called a *project organization,* which is a self-sufficient division to handle a new activity or an unusually complex product. Such a format, which may be temporary, is popular in the defense industry.

A logical extension of the marketing point of view is the *market* or *industry organization,* in which the company is organized to serve specified customer markets with one or a multiplicity of product lines. Focusing on the marketplace has caused many dramatic reorganizations in large, diversified U.S. companies during the past decade, including the much-talked-about one at General Electric. Many observers think GE's Strategic Business Units presage another wave of restructuring, especially in multinational companies.

Finally, there are *combination complex organizations* with a basic functional organization, geographic organization for marketing and manufacturing, a group executive or two for all corporate staffs, a separate product division (complete with marketing, manufacturing, and staffs), and a separate market-based division.

relating strategy and structure

Regardless of what most textbooks say, organization design should start with the marketplace and be dominated by the chosen corporate strategy. "Businesses are structured to carry out strategies in the markets they serve. It follows that as market conditions evolve, as strategies are reshaped, and as customer groups change in character, organization structure must change accordingly."[6]

[6] E. Raymond Corey and Steven H. Star, *Organization Strategy: A Marketing Approach* (Cambridge, Mass.: Harvard University Press, 1971), p. 1.

Relating strategy and structure is an iterative process. As recent studies have documented, organization structure usually follows strategy;[7] however, the organization design and the power structure embodied within it help determine how the business will respond to perceived market opportunities and choose among alternate strategies. "Today's organization is an important influence molding tomorrow's strategy which in turn shapes tomorrow's organization."[8]

The linking of market–strategy–structure has produced an entirely new way of viewing organizational structure and its continuing evolution. To understand this most dramatic conceptual shift, its importance for strategy implementation, the new organizational format appearing in the 1970s, and the logical reasons for large companies to constantly restructure, one must review briefly the salient points in recent industrial organization history.

INITIAL RESPONSES: A HISTORICAL PERSPECTIVE

Until the 1880s and 1890s, most of the businesses in the United States were single-product companies, and whatever organization design existed was simple.[9] Typically, a firm began as a one-man family company and gradually expanded to include two top managers: a general superintendent personally overseeing the laboring force and a president or treasurer who handled finances, purchasing, and relations with the commission sales agents. Few manufacturing firms marketed their own products.

Sheer increases in volume brought change and the absorption of additional functions. Firms employing relatively new technology (such as meatpacking or electrical machinery) often found existing distribution channels unsatisfactory and so created their own marketing organizations. Both Westinghouse and General Electric followed this approach and even included subdepartments for each major product area within both sales and engineering. Other companies with more staple products (such as textiles or oil) combined horizontally and either ab-

---

[7] Alfred D. Chandler, Jr., *Strategy and Structure: Chapters on the History of the American Industrial Enterprise* (Cambridge, Mass.: M.I.T. Press, 1962), pp. 14–16.

[8] Corey and Star, op. cit., p. 51.

[9] Some of this historical perspective is drawn from Chandler, op. cit., pp. 19–51.

figure one

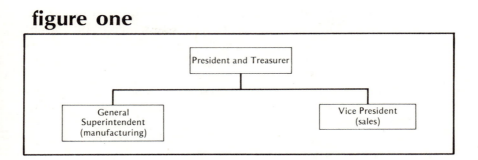

sorbed or were absorbed by their sales agents. Many integrated backward into making some of their own supplies.

Whatever the route, the addition of new activities forced increased structuring of the organization. Instead of two executives working together, often as equal partners, the new organization appeared as in Figure 1.

The jolt of decreasing status for the general superintendent was often greater than indicated by Figure 1. Many presidents, especially those directing soft-goods companies, soon discovered how vital the newly acquired marketing function was and began to compensate the sales manager or vice president considerably more than his manufacturing counterpart.

The rapid business expansion of the 1880s and 1890s brought more consolidation and vertical integration (into purchasing, transportation, and raw material supplies) and the burgeoning of the departmental form of organization. Steel, fertilizer, oil, paper, rubber, and other companies that experienced rapid departmentalization had a partial model to follow—the Pennsylvania Railroad. A generation earlier, transportation companies had faced the need for structuring varied activities and had developed the concept of line and staff, with the former responsible for people and the latter for things (such as rolling stock). The Pennsylvania had gone further and evolved the concept of the departmental vice president responsible for long-run strategy and the general manager responsible for day-to-day operations.

Industrial firms, dealing as they did with more numerous and more complex activities than just transportation, found the Pennsylvania tough to imitate. Between 1896 and 1920, the largest firms evolved from holding companies to highly centralized, functionally departmentalized structures. Power and control were concentrated in a few functional heads at headquarters who usually were too busy with area administrative problems to worry much about the long run or the corporation as a whole. The Pennsylvania's vice president concept was yet to become a reality elsewhere.

Some industries continued to sell the same products to the same types of customers down through the 1960s. For most metals, sugar, meat, and liquor companies, for example, the centralized, functional form of organization still made a great deal of sense.

innovative response: the multidivisional organization

Other companies diversified—either through internal growth or through acquisition—and during the 1920s the multidivisional form of organization evolved. In its purest form, the organization chart resembled a splitting amoeba—each new product meant adding a new, self-contained division that often was operated more like an independent company than a subsidiary. Each new product had its own manufacturing, sales, administration, and often R&D departments. Such an organization meant that products could be added or dropped without disturbing the overall corporate structure, and permitted tight coordination and control within each product group; however, controlling the often disparate divisions for the overall corporate good was another matter.

The problem with such an organization was the lack of any economies from the diversification. Aside from the access to capital—often no mean advantage—the division or subsidiary had no real economic advantage over its independent, separate counterpart. Indeed, the division had the disadvantage of having to subscribe to corporate overhead.

The solution was the pooling of functional areas common to all product divisions where sufficient commonality of interest and skills existed. Typically, R&D was the first area to be pooled, since often the work done was common to several products (e.g., a group of chemicals, plastics, or automobiles). The second area to be combined was often manufacturing, again because the problems and skills involved gradually merged. Accounting usually preceded or immediately followed manufacturing; the usefulness of having a coordinated, standardized flow of quantitative data for the monitoring of performance and, later, budgeting became increasingly obvious as firms became larger and more diverse.

Sales or marketing was the last area to be pooled, and then often only at the vocal behest of customers. The impetus was external to the organization rather than internal. When a company's products become mature (as opposed to new items or technical specialties) and a number of products are sold to each customer, the latter soon urges his suppliers to have one salesman call on him.

The pooling of a sales force raised a new problem: coordination of functional areas—especially manufacturing and sales—by *product line*. If manufacturing is pooled, so that all products are jumbled together, and sales is pooled, so that each salesman sells all the firm's products, then who coordinates the manufacturing and sales of any one product? The answer is the product manager, perhaps the most controversial figure of large, multidivisional, multinational American corporations.[10] He might be the former *line* manager for a single product, who had both sales and manufacturing reporting to him. Now he is a *staff* person with responsibility but little or no authority for the coordination and sales success of the same product. How much of that product is actually sold used to depend on his orders but now depends on the ease of sale and the product manager's persuasive powers. After all, why shouldn't a salesman with a broad product line sell either what the customer asks for or what is easiest to sell?

world war II: experimentation from necessity

World War II interrupted much speculation about the product manager concept and provoked even more drastic innovations. Managers started to discard the old rules and organize to emphasize company skills, maximize the use of scarce resources, or shore up weaknesses. Consolidated Vultee Aircraft is a case in point.[11]

Consolidated Aircraft and Vultee were to merge in 1943 and

[10] And controversy there is: The defections of PepsiCo, Eastman Kodak, Levi Strauss, Heublein, and others are detailed in "The Brand Manager: No Longer King," *Business Week*, June 9, 1973, pp. 58–66.

[11] For a complete description of the organizational changes, see "Consolidated Vultee Aircraft Corporation (A)," (BP427R-A). Copyright 1946 by the President and Fellows of Harvard College.

become one of the world's largest producers of aircraft (including the B-24, or "Liberator"); with 1941 sales of $140 million and 30,000 employees, they were beyond the control of a one-man president-founder. At the behest of the military, ownership changed hands and Tom Girdler, the tough executive who had put Republic Steel together, took charge. As *Fortune* commented, "there were no brass bands or welcoming committees waiting for Tom Girdler."[12]

Mr. Girdler merged the two associated companies and banged heads together. The resulting organization chart (borrowed from Republic Steel) is shown in Exhibit 1. The seven "staff" departments had direct responsibility for their functional areas; they could issue direct orders both to the 12 division managers and to their division-level functional counterparts. The latter were supposed to keep their bosses informed of any direct orders from headquarters. The division managers were held completely responsible to top management for the operating results of their divisions; conflicts between the division manager and the staff people were to be settled between them; in the rare instances in which this was not possible, top management would arbitrate.

The theory behind such an organization was that the seven staff departments would function as a "general manager's office" and optimize the performance of each function, coordinate all functions, keep both top and division management informed, and standardize operation and control procedures. Thus, the "president's office" was expanded while the division manager was left responsible for local coordination, feedback, and airplane output.

What really made this work was the unifying wartime goal of getting planes out. The structure maximized the effectiveness of the scarcest resource (the top functional managers) while providing a clear goal and standard for the division manager (the number of planes per hour). In fact, the division manager was really a *product manager* and the staff people were functional (or resource) *line managers*. And like the product manager, the division manager had lots of responsibility but little authority: only his leadership and persuasive skills![13]

[12] "Tom Girdler's Truce," *Fortune* 26, no. 3 (September 1942): 89.

[13] Some argue that such an organization would work effectively only in wartime, when there were strong, unifying shared values—and direct "staff" control was eliminated in 1945. Others maintain that the situation resembles any outfit with a strong staff.

exhibit one

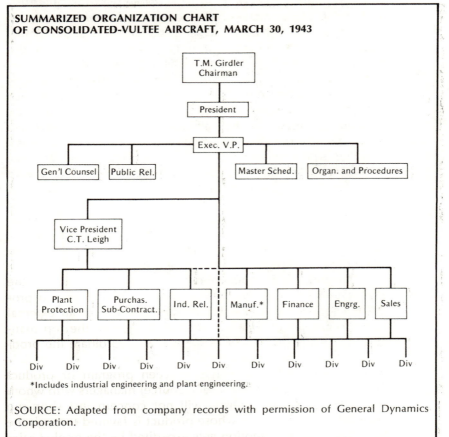

SUMMARIZED ORGANIZATION CHART OF CONSOLIDATED-VULTEE AIRCRAFT, MARCH 30, 1943

*Includes industrial engineering and plant engineering.

SOURCE: Adapted from company records with permission of General Dynamics Corporation.

the postwar years: the rise of the product manager

For some consumer goods companies, such as Proctor and Gamble, the product manager antedated World War II; for most, however, this position is a recent innovation. He is usually in charge of one or more product programs, which are really strategic plans for serving a particular market segment. The programs include policies and plans for the entire marketing mix: product design, distribution channels, advertising, promotion, field selling, price, physical distribution, and customer service.

If the product manager was forced on some companies by their customers, universal acceptance came with the fuller understanding of the marketing concept that businesses exist to service customer needs, not to sell products. Hence, the identification of a *customer segment,* not a product line, became the starting point for organization design. Once understood, organizing around market segments to serve customer needs rather than around products to be sold spawned a new wave of major reorganizations.

Product programs are typically combined into administrative units called product departments, divisions, or businesses. These units have an integrated set of resources to plan and implement one or more programs, and are of sufficient size to maximize (hopefully) the economies of scale and specialization in manufacturing, distribution, and research. Usually, the products are related by common markets, technology, materials base, manufacturing processes, distribution channels, managerial knowledge or skills, or some combination of these. These relationships are shown in matrix form in Exhibit 2.[14]

Such a matrix highlights some of the conflicts inherent in the new framework. Clearly, there will be conflicts between programs about the use of internal resources and about external relationships with customers. Part of the job of the top management of the division or business is to coordinate the product programs and adjudicate the conflicts.

There will also be conflicts between program or product managers and the functional (or resource) managers with whom they interact. These conflicts will not concern just short-run resource allocation (e.g., whose product is favored through the factory or which promotion gets expedited by the pooled sales force), but strategy as well. Resource or functional managers tend to form strategies that will use and develop *existing* skills and resources, while product program managers are tied to the markets served and usually push for *new* products, resources, skills—in other words, change.[15]

An excellent illustration of a firm that went from a single-product organization to a complex product manager structure is the Textile Fibers Department (or area) of E. I. du Pont de Nemours.

[14] Corey and Star, op. cit., p. 8.
[15] Ibid., p. 5.

exhibit two

RESOURCE AND PROGRAM MANAGEMENT INTERFACES

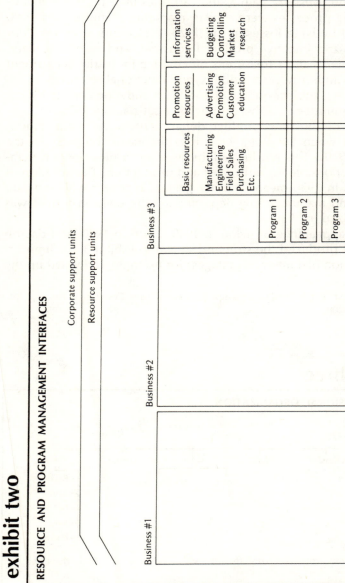

SOURCE: Adapted from E. Raymond Corey and Steven H. Star, *Organization Strategy: A Marketing Approach* (Cambridge, Mass.: Harvard University Press, 1971, pp. 3–4. Copyright 1971 by the President and Fellows of Harvard College.

THE DU PONT EXAMPLE

Du Pont started as a gunpowder manufacturer, but with the loss of government orders in 1908 the firm rapidly branched out.[16] Artificial leather and celluloid products were added in 1910, and dyestuffs, paints, and varnishes in 1917. While manufacturing processes were similar, marketing definitely was not. Spurred by large losses in the 1920–1921 depression, Du Pont reorganized into five product (industrial) and eight (auxiliary) departments and a treasurer's office. Each industrial department had the authority, responsibility, and functional resources to run a business, subject only to the recommendations of the executive committee and the earning of a satisfactory ROI.

One of the new product departments was Textile Fibers, formed when Du Pont went into the rayon business in the early 1920s. This product addition meant a new general manager responsible for both sales and production. The addition of acetate in 1930 meant another general manager with separate sales and manufacturing departments; the division format was formalized in 1936.

The appearance of nylon in 1939, orlon in 1950, and dacron in 1951 produced the structure shown in Exhibit 3. Such an organization had many advantages; for example, it divided up the

[16] Most of the Du Pont example is drawn from Corey and Star, op. cit., pp. 187–200.

exhibit three

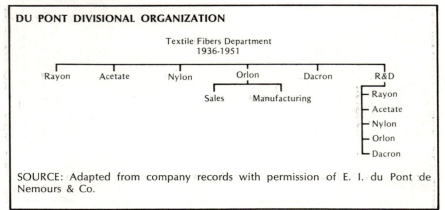

DU PONT DIVISIONAL ORGANIZATION

Textile Fibers Department
1936-1951

Rayon Acetate Nylon Orlon Dacron R&D

Sales Manufacturing

— Rayon
— Acetate
— Nylon
— Orlon
— Dacron

SOURCE: Adapted from company records with permission of E. I. du Pont de Nemours & Co.

business task around the key job (production) and the scarcest resource (production capacity), provided for clearly defined responsibility and coordination of manufacturing and sales, facilitated the addition or deletion of businesses (as was subsequently done with rayon) without disturbing the other products, and encouraged management thinking and control systems to focus on specific products.

Such an organization worked effectively as long as the Textile Fibers Department's customers—the weaving mills—typically bought only one fiber; product and customer were synonymous. However, when the "battle of the fibers" turned into the "marriage of the fibers" during 1950–1951, the structure rapidly became dysfunctional. Division managers started to make optimistic forecasts for their fiber at the expense of other divisions and to compete for capital expenditure dollars. More important, as customers began blending fibers and thus using more than one, they complained about having to deal with several Du Pont salesmen.

functional organization

The response to such pressures was to consolidate the five divisions into the traditional functional format with one sales department, one manufacturing department, and one research department. (See Exhibit 4.) Each of these departments, however, was organized along product lines. For example, for each fiber there were separate manufacturing facilities, separate R&D teams, and a separate sales force. Still, the fact that sales and manufacturing each reported to a single head ensured increased functional control.

One major change was the addition of Technical Sales (partly removed from the R&D arm). Within it, the sales development group worked with weavers, finishers, and cutters (apparel manufacturers) to find new uses for man-made fibers. The technical service group concentrated on customer problems.

The functional consolidation was a transitional format that sufficed until the sales force was trained to handle all five fibers. The shift to a product manager form of organization was hastened by depressed market conditions.

product/market manager organization

The introduction of six merchandising division managers in 1954 dramatically changed the organization. (See Exhibit 5.) The

exhibit four

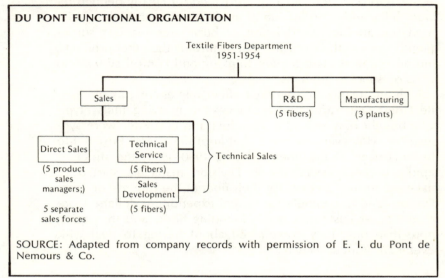

DU PONT FUNCTIONAL ORGANIZATION

Textile Fibers Department
1951-1954

Sales — R&D (5 fibers) — Manufacturing (3 plants)

Direct Sales — Technical Service (5 fibers) — Sales Development (5 fibers) } Technical Sales

Direct Sales
(5 product sales managers;)

5 separate sales forces

SOURCE: Adapted from company records with permission of E. I. du Pont de Nemours & Co.

exhibit five

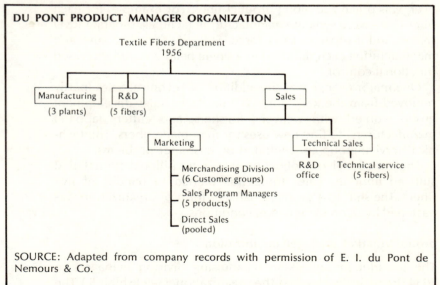

DU PONT PRODUCT MANAGER ORGANIZATION

Textile Fibers Department
1956

Manufacturing (3 plants) — R&D (5 fibers) — Sales

Marketing — Technical Sales

Marketing:
— Merchandising Division (6 Customer groups)
— Sales Program Managers (5 products)
— Direct Sales (pooled)

Technical Sales:
R&D office — Technical service (5 fibers)

SOURCE: Adapted from company records with permission of E. I. du Pont de Nemours & Co.

merchandising division was organized by *customer groups* (men's wear, women's wear, home furnishings, and industrial) and by function (marketing research and advertising). Each of the customer groups was subdivided—for example, men's wear was split into boy's wear, furnishings and sportswear, tailored outerwear, and utility clothing.

Merchandise (or market) managers had two main functions: (1) developing marketing plans to meet customers' fiber needs and (2) promoting Du Pont-brand fibers. Both jobs required close and continuing relationships at all levels of the textile industry.

The technical sales area was changed by moving the R&D division's textile and industrial product research group to sales and substituting it for the disbanded sales development group. The new group did applications research on the uses of Du Pont fibers in specific end products.

Two years later the transition was to a product manager form of organization. This step entailed the establishment of a pooled multifiber sales force; henceforth, marketing efforts were focused on customer end-use needs, not fibers. In some cases, salespeople were specialized by industry; for example, an Akron salesperson sold only to rubber companies, another in New York handled only rope and cordage accounts, while a third in Philadelphia specialized in thread manufacturers.

Some coordination by fiber was still necessary, however, and therefore a sales program division manager (or product program manager) was appointed for each fiber. This was a staff job coordinating the various marketing departments with each other and with the manufacturing plants. Sales program managers, for example, had major responsibility for inventory levels and worked on scheduling production, planning new plant capacity, developing new products and uses, and sales promotion in end-use markets.

evaluation of organizational change

In retrospect, Du Pont's Textile Fibers Department traversed the gamut of organization formats. It started as a single-product department (rayon). The addition of acetate in 1930 proved indigestible, so the separate division approach was adopted in 1936. Further product additions brought more divisions and no economies; hence the replacement of product division heads with resource managers (manufacturing and sales) in 1951.

The restructuring might have ended there except that Du Pont completely changed its strategy from selling products to servicing markets and customer needs. Hence the shift to merchandising managers (market or end-use program managers) and sales program (product) managers. The causes for the shift were multiple, including the maturing of the product line, the rapid drop in technical and production problems, the decreasing customer need for product education, the rise of blends, the flowering of competition, industry overcapacity, and the need for total fiber forecasts and planning. Most of all, Du Pont wanted to develop selective demand for its brands as well as building primary demand for man-mades. This meant selling at all levels of the distribution chain, not just the weavers.[17]

One result was that the interfiber competition that had emerged in the customers' waiting room shifted to the sales program managers. The need for coordination moved from the *external* world to the *internal* one.

Another result was to raise the level of the pricing decision in the organization. Previously, each division manager had priced his own fiber, since there was little fiber competition. Under the new setup, basic price levels were determined by the top management of the Textile Fibers Department, with the sales division manager responsible for new-product pricing. The latter solicited the recommendations of the sales program managers.

STRATEGY AND STRUCTURE OVERSEAS

The progression from geographic to product line to market-centered organization is not limited to domestic U.S. corporations; the same trends are clear overseas. A discussion of Monsanto's overseas experience between 1954 and 1967 will be illustrative.[18]

Between 1954 and 1967, Monsanto's international operations changed from a small, relatively independent foreign subsidiary and export operation to a directly controlled arm of the domestic product divisions. In fact, to some observers the future of the International Division as such seems in jeopardy.

---

[17] Expansion of the product line and the rise of international activity prompted further evolution to a *market based* profit center organization with responsibility for technical activities, manufacturing and marketing within each. The first profit center division was established in 1969 for Nomex spunbonded products that involved different technology, manufactu-

Foreign operations resembled a stepchild during most of the period from 1920 to 1934. Monsanto made its first overseas investment (in Wales) in 1920, and added two more (in Canada and Australia) by 1939, when a foreign department was formed to handle the limited export sales. The overseas acquisitions were separate, independent businesses; the only link with the domestic operation was the licensing and interchange of technical information.

geographic organization

As Monsanto invested in 19 foreign countries between 1950 and 1954 and export sales multiplied, the old complete decentralization system faltered; conflicts arose with the rapid increase in volume and products, and the need for coordination became apparent. In 1954, the Overseas Division replaced the Foreign Department and was given a mandate to manage Monsanto's overseas investments. For the first six years the organization was on a broad area basis, with one director of sales for the Western Hemisphere and one for the Eastern Hemisphere. Each supervised an organization structured along product lines cor-

---

ing processes, and new markets for DuPont. By 1974, the department had evolved as follows:

Textile Fibers Department

1974

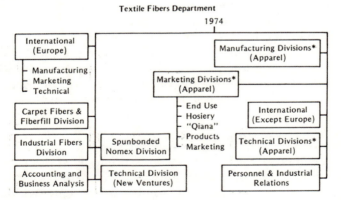

*Divisional General Directors have a coordinating responsibility across the department in their respective functions. "Apparel" also includes home furnishings.

SOURCE: Adapted from company records with permission of E.I. du Pont de Nemours & Co.

[18] Most of the Monsanto example is drawn from Corey and Star, op. cit., pp. 370–389.

responding to the existing operating divisions (organic and inorganic). Plastic sales, which were organized on a worldwide basis, were an exception.

product line organization

Then, in 1961, Monsanto shifted to a product line approach, with directors of sales for organic, inorganic–agricultural, and plastics on an international basis. Within each group the field forces were grouped geographically.

The reasons for these shifts from area to product organization seem clear. An area basis seems simplest when faced with strange environments and urgent coordination needs—the route Monsanto's rival Dow has taken overseas. Such a structure reduces the amount of detailed decision making forced upward because it assumes that strategy and coordination problems are strictly regional. On the other hand, the product line format indicated that customers, competition, and prices were rapidly becoming worldwide. With the domestic organization on a product line basis and the U.S. divisions becoming more interested in world markets, the shift seemed natural.

Two years later, in 1963, Monsanto created Monsanto Europe, but since the largest subsidiary (in the U.K.) and Chemstrand were omitted and the new organization was really given only consultative powers, the shift proved mere window dressing.

Conflicts mounted. Member companies intensified competition with each other and with domestic divisions in world markets. There was a noticeable lack of sales and technical coordination with large international customers. Worst of all, when supplies were short, domestic divisions favored domestic customers; the reverse was true during oversupply situations.

assignment of profit responsibility

In 1964, there was a clear break as domestic divisions were given worldwide profit responsibility for their products. Divisional managers were supposed to plan and execute worldwide product strategies. The new International Division was to "administer" overseas activities and act as an advisory staff by contributing foreign market expertise. In fact, the International Division quickly went beyond providing the assigned "initiative and coordination" of worldwide strategies and became actively involved in strategy formulation, with operating divisions taking a more passive role. International managers felt the need for strong commercial development groups to be sure the domestic divisions were aware of and capitalized on overseas opportunities.

The conflict between product strategy and area organization became sharper. As one manager said, "what's best for the product strategy is not always best for Monsanto in each country. Part of ID's responsibility is to see that the country organization remains strong as product strategies are developed and implemented."[19]

conflict resolution

The untenable situation in which the domestic divisions were charged with profit responsibility but not prepared to assume it, while the International Division was giving up nothing, came to a head with the appointment of a new general manager for the International Division in 1967. The new charter called on the operating divisions to "prepare market and customer strategies using data, information and area market strategies provided by the International Division for the ex-U.S. portions." As for the International Division, it was to develop "total business plans and profit goals for each member company based on the profit plans established by the operating divisions." Operating divisions were to initiate and make overseas capital investments, while ID was to control organization structures and manpower and to "safeguard the investment in member companies abroad."[20]

Clearly, the International Division was to develop and preserve resources to carry out strategies initiated by the product divisions. To do this the division had to be sure the proposed strategies were viable and would not put member companies in jeopardy. The international marketing managers were functioning as geographic extensions of the market product management teams at headquarters with respect to strategy. Henceforth, the Monsanto product division would provide worldwide, not regional, strategies.

What about the future? How will this—or any multinational organization—evolve? One possibility is the dissolution of the International Division. More likely, the International Division will continue as specialized, local resource managers who implement regional strategies. If international organizations are

[19] Corey and Star, op. cit., p. 374.
[20] Ibid.

following the normal pattern of going from area to product segmentation, then will not the progression continue to market or end-use segmentation?

other overseas examples

Lest the Monsanto example seem at all unique in that structure followed strategy, further research among the "Fortune 500" and the largest manufacturing firms in the United Kingdom, France, Germany, and Italy between 1950 and 1970 demonstrated dramatically that growth via diversification has become the most common strategy in Europe as well as in the United States. "Increasing diversity plus competitive pressures seem to be forcing European companies to adopt the divisional structure, as they have the large companies in the United States."[21]

This divisional structure seems to be shifting from geographic to worldwide product responsibility. The fourth-largest company outside of the United States, Philips Lamp, is a case in point. Its nationally based, geographic organization made sense before the formation of the Common Market; having self-contained plants in each country serving only local markets enabled Philips to respond to local needs and maintain national identity. EEC tariff cutting ruined his advantage, but it was not until 1972 that the organizational shift to specialized plants serving many countries showed a financial return.[22] By 1974, both ITT and Continental Oil had "world product managers."

GENERAL ELECTRIC AND THE SBU CONCEPT

General Electric approached the 1970s with a severe problem: excessive operating decentralization. This had not always been the case. Back in 1948, for example, any pay increase that raised an exempt salary to more than $6000 annually had to have the chief executive's approval. Ralph Cordiner established the concept of decentralization with virtually self-contained businesses as building blocks in the early 1950s. But by 1967, growth plus far-flung diversification had made the old business structure too large and cumbersome to cope with increasing risk and outside consumer pressures.

[21] Bruce R. Scott, "The Industrial State: Old Myths and New Realities," *Harvard Business Review 51*, no. 2 (March–April 1973): 141.

[22] "Philips: A Multinational Copes with Profitless Growth," *Business Week*, January 13, 1973, pp. 64–65.

Thus, in 1968, the president's office was expanded to 5 people, the 5 groups enlarged to 10, the 29 divisions reorganized into 50, and the 110 departments split into 170. "The whole thrust was to put in place components of a size, complexity, and span that a manager could better get his arms around from a management control standpoint."[23] However, in the proliferation of businesses the concept of a department being not only a profit center but a self-contained business was often lost, and the problem of ensuring that adequate attention was given to long-range planning became critical.

The solution was (1) separating operations from strategy at the corporate staff level by assigning the former to the corporate administrative staff and the latter to the corporate executive staff, and (2) superimposing on the operating group, division, and departmental structure some 43 new components called Strategic Business Units (SBUs). Each SBU had to have clearly identified competition and "the ability to accomplish integrated strategic planning on markets, products, services, facilities and organizations with relatively slight concern for the actions or results of other SBU's"[24] but within the context of overall corporate strategy.

Put another way, enough of the following requirements had to be fulfilled "to realistically focus total business accountability, both short and long range, in one manager":

1. The component must have a unique business mission independent of the mission of any other component.
2. The component must have a clearly identified set of competitors.
3. The component must be a full-fledged competitor in the external market (as contrasted with a dominant role as an internal supplier).
4. The component must have the ability to accomplish integrated Strategic Planning with respect to products, markets, facilities, and organization, relatively independent of other SBUs.
5. The component manager must be able to "call the shots" (within approved plans) on the areas crucial to the success of that particular business including as a minimum: technology, manufacturing, marketing, and cash management.[25]

SBUs can be at any level. For example, aerospace, aircraft engines, and major appliances are SBUs at the group level,

[23] "GE's Evolving Management System," January 18, 1972, pp. 3–4. (Internal presentation, quoted with permission of General Electric Co.)

[24] McKitterick, op. cit., p. 3.

[25] "GE's Evolving Management System," op. cit., pp. 6–7.

while medical systems, appliance components, and contractor equipment SBUs are at the division level and tungsten carbide tooling and wiring devices are at the department level. Initially, a very few, such as monochrome TV, were at the still-lower business section echelon; however, by 1974 there were none at that level. According to Herman L. Weiss, vice chairman and executive officer, "what makes an SBU is the level where the strategic business decisions are made—where it all comes together.[26]

As for reporting, most SBU managers were formerly divisional vice presidents and hence enjoy high status. Their strategies are reviewed by the echelon above. For example, if a component (department, division, or group) becomes an SBU, it performs the strategic planning function, while if it becomes part of an SBU, it does operational planning. If a component is above an SBU, it performs the strategy review function. While group and division managers typically have staff with some title such as "Manager, Group Strategic Planning and Review Operation," department level SBU managers may do their own planning. In any case, the SBU manager is ultimately responsible for his SBU's strategic plans, and his performance is evaluated on adherance to those plans, not on short term profits. Reginald H. Jones, Chairman of the Board and Chief Executive Officer, explains, "It's our job to reach agreement with the SBU manager and to convince him that if he stays on the strategy and realizes his targets—whether they are to divest certain product lines or move ahead on a growth strategy—that we will recognize that he has implemented the strategy successfully." However, Mr. Jones is quick to add that matching managers and strategies is difficult, especially for businesses to be harvested and those marked for divestiture. "We're all sort of Churchillian in nature. None of us wants to liquidate the empire. . . ."[27]

According to General Electric, the results have heightened management's ability to do portfolio management (see Chapter 3) by focusing the resource allocation process on 43 clearly identified businesses or SBU's instead of on 170 departments. Resources are put into product areas that have (or clearly have the potential for) a large share in high-growth industries, while mature products in slower-growing industries are "harvested" for cash. As for products with low shares and profits in slow-

---

[26] "GE's New Strategy for Faster Growth," *Business Week,* July 8, 1972, p. 56.

[27] *Business Week,* op. cit., p. 58.

growth industries, they are sold; for example, the TV broadcasting equipment business was sold in July 1972.

INCREASING SOPHISTICATION: FURTHER CHANGE AND RESPONSES

As any reader of the business press—or even annual reports—knows, large-scale organizations are continuing to change. Sometimes a business unit gets too big and must split up or decentralize—as Du Pont did in 1921 and many others have since. The main impetus to change is pinpointing new markets or new products that end up requiring partial or complete specialization. Hence, organizations with product managers and pooled sales suddenly go through a tumultuous upheaval as all or part of the sales force is specialized again. Markets are segmented by products, end uses, buyer behavior patterns, and geography; program managers may focus on any one of these segments, depending on which aspect of marketing strategy is most critical. Generally, geographic segmentation gives way to product orientation and in turn yields to end-use or buyer behavior schemes.[28] This process is endless: As markets change, strategies change, and so must organization structure.

The need for still another coordinating activity forces change in complex organizations. That need is for the independent scheduling function, such as Mobil's Supply, Distribution and Traffic Department located in neither the resource nor the program structure, that "matches demand in a wide range of markets with limited resources and products at maximum profit."[29] Such scheduling managers must be especially objective and tough, for they are the "traffic cops" who say *what* ought to be made and *who* should get it.

With all the layering of product program managers and market program managers in complex organizations, the overall strategy for serving a specified market may get lost. Hence, the General Electric SBU concept is getting much careful attention in other large companies, both within and outside of the electrical industry. For example, in 1973 General Foods adopted the concept and substituted five marketing SBU's (Breakfast, Beverage, Main Meal, Dessert, and Pet Food) for the traditional grocery product divisions (Birds Eye, Jell-O, Post, and Kool-Aid). Production, sales, personnel, market research, and most new

---

[28] Corey and Star, op. cit., p. 47.
[29] Ibid., p. 47.

product development were consolidated either at the corporate or divisional level, leaving the SBU's with "pure" marketing activities and needed support.[30] Then, in February, 1975, Westinghouse grouped its 120 divisions into 37 "basic business units." Strategic planning of market growth and capital expansion will be coordinated at the business unit level instead of in the divisional profit centers.[31]

The SBU manager is really the equivalent of the chief executive officer of a company interfacing with a clearly defined market. But in the GE version, he also has line responsibility over all operating components necessary for his operation. (In case of two SBU's needing one resource, the resource is usually assigned to where the strategic importance is greatest.) Generally, SBU general managers do not report to another SBU manager at a higher level because no strategic business unit is part of any other one. A division made up of a number of departmental level SBU's is classified as a multibusiness division and has the strategy review responsibility with respect to the department SBU's.

One seemingly surprising result is that a person no longer has to be a multifunctional generalist with a flair for strategy in order to become a general manager. Departments and divisions not designated as SBU's continue to be headed by general managers responsible for operations. In addition, there are functional divisions (such as aircraft engine manufacturing or engineering) headed by general managers reporting to a group executive.

The explicit relating of strategy to organizational structure is a process that is clearly in its infancy. As more and more companies see the necessity for changing both organization structure and strategy as markets change, the number of changes and variations from "orthodox" arrangements should increase. However, making explicit the tight connection between markets, strategy, and structure should help explain to operating managers, especially in multinational corporations, why the reorganizations may seem almost constant. And doubtless there are strategies now being conceived that will change dramatically the organizations of the next decade.

---

[30] "The Rebuilding Job at General Foods," *Business Week*, August 25, 1973, p. 51.

[31] "Westinghouse Opts for a GE Pattern," *Business Week*, February 3, 1975, pp. 18–19.

six

FUTURE CHALLENGES: PINPOINTING OPPORTUNITIES AND STRATEGY IMPLEMENTATION

The next decade should provide some answers to at least two areas of business policy that need better conceptual frameworks. These are (1) the pinpointing of future opportunities and (2) the implementation of strategy, starting with the identification of the company, divisional, departmental, or individual task assignment. This chapter will review the past history, current practices, and future prospects of each topic and dispel some myths in the process.

PINPOINTING OPPORTUNITIES

Environmental analysis and forecasting may well receive the most attention of any business policy topic in the near future, and for good reason. As readers of Alvin Toffler's *Future Shock* know full well, change is occurring with "ever accelerating speed," is having "unprecedented impact," and will pose severe problems of adaptation. According to Toffler, the probable "mass disorientation" is caused by the superimposition of new cultures on old ones at a dizzyingly accelerated pace.[1] Whether one agrees with Toffler or not, the daily paper and the out-cries of special-interest groups and young Americans attest to the rate of change and its pervasiveness.

During the mid-1960s the business press reflected the increasing concern with forecasting change in the environment. Typically, such trend analysis and projections are based on four seemingly separable environmental segments: economic, social, political, and technological.

[1] Alvin Toffler, *Future Shock* (New York: Bantam, 1970), pp. 9–11.

economic trends

Economic projections are the most numerous, and with the aid of the computer, the number and accuracy of such forecasts have increased. Companies use published forecasts (such as the regular and extensive ones made by the National Planning Association), commission an outside consultant, or employ an in-house economist.

Some industries, such as life insurance, are both directly and immediately affected by economic shifts: For example, the tight money squeeze in the fall of 1966 produced severe cash flow problems as prepayments dropped off and policy loans rose rapidly. Some companies resorted to substantial short-term borrowings, while others liquidated capital investments (often at a loss). However, December 1971 saw the reverse, with the industry embarrassingly "cash heavy" and looking for borrowers.

Many companies and products are affected only indirectly by day-to-day or even long-term economic shifts. A company may compile in a "war room" or present at a board meeting a whole raft of macroeconomic indexes, but revert to straightforward market research for planning purposes. For example, in 1968 a major TV manufacturer proudly presented its computer-aided five-year forecasts. After a series of basic economic indicators, the presentation turned to predicting price and volume levels and relied mainly on the traditional industry yardsticks (such as the number of households, TV homes at year end, an assumed ten-year set survival curve, dealer and distributor inventory ratios, the degradation of component prices, etc.). Economic trends served merely as a backdrop and a check on the "built-up" forecast.

Still, larger companies are going further and consulting econometricians who build models of the economy. There are many in the business besides the federal government—for example, Wharton Econometric Forecasting Associates (the non-profit firm that evolved from the post-World War II Lawrence Klein–Arthur Goldberger model that first predicted the course of the U.S. economy); Chase Econometric Associates (a bank subsidiary founded by an associate of Professor Klein); the Brookings Institution; Data Resources (founded in 1969 by Harvard's Otto Eckstein); and GE's Mapcast, aimed at "the intelligent company vice president" of medium-sized firms rather than the large company technical specialist. Annual fees range from $2,520 to $20,000.[2]

social and political trends

While men like Jules Verne, H. G. Wells, and Aldous Huxley have provided the most memorable visionary fantasies, the current crop of "futurologists," with their more disciplined and earnest projections of the sociopolitical world, should have more impact on public and private decision making. In fact, the 1960s saw futurology (as it is called) become something of a fad because of the proliferation of practitioners. Best known is Herman Kahn, director of the Hudson Institute in Croton-on-Hudson, New York.

Dr. Kahn specializes in writing scenarios in order to see how the future may evolve as a logical sequence of events. Although his book *The Year 2000* contained the most startling projections and made him much in demand as a lecturer, his warnings about the growing economic power of Japan in *The Emerging Japanese Superstate* reinforced business fears and earned him top-management attention.[3] Less startling but sobering is his portrait of the world of the 1970s and 1980s in *Things to Come.* As he points out, "thinking about the future can tell us a lot about the present."[4]

Two other tools used by a sociopolitical forecasting leader, General Electric, are the "Probability-Diffusion Matrix" and the "Values Profile." In the matrix, each predicted event is placed with the degree of probability (low to high) in the x-axis and the degree of diffusion (uniform distribution over the applicable population) on the y-axis. In the values profile, contrasting pairs of values (war vs. peace, conformity vs. pluralism) are shown to a trend-setting population segment (young, well-educated, relatively affluent, "committed"). Comparing the balance struck today with a hypothetical one for, say, 1980, may help predict value trends, but not necessarily events.[5]

[2] *Wall Street Journal,* August 23, 1972, pp. 1, 23.

[3] Herman Kahn and Anthony J. Wiener, *The Year 2000* (New York: Macmillan, 1967), and Herman Kahn, *The Emerging Japanese Superstate* (New York: Macmillan, 1970).

[4] Herman Kahn and B. Bruce-Briggs, *Things to Come* (New York: Macmillan, 1972), p. 2.

[5] Ian H. Wilson, "Socio-Political Forecasting: A New Dimension to Strategic Planning," *Michigan Business Review 26,* no. 4, (July 1974): 15–25.

technological trends

The escalation of technological change is clearly evident in the world around us. To cite an oft-repeated example:

> If the last 50,000 years of man's existence were divided into 800 lifetimes of some 62 years each, about 650 were spent in caves, until the last 70 there was no effective written communication, only the last six saw the printed word, only the last four measured time with any accuracy, the last two used an electric motor, and the 800th lifetime saw most of today's products invented. In fact, 90 percent of all the scientists who ever lived are now alive and the lead time for the commercial application of an innovation is often months—not the 100 years for the combine or 150 years for the typewriter.[6]

Often it's hard to realize the speed of this change, since it is occurring all around us. For example, in 1946 Rand reported on the question of satellites:

> Although the crystal ball is cloudy, two things seem clear—
> 1. A satellite vehicle with appropriate instrumentation can be expected to be one of the most potent scientific tools of the Twentieth Century.
> 2. The achievement of a satellite craft by the United States would inflame the imagination of mankind, and would probably produce repercussions in the world comparable to the explosion of the atomic bomb. . . .
>
> Since mastery of the elements is a reliable index of material progress, the nation which first makes significant achievements in space travel will be acknowledged as the world leader in both military and scientific techniques. To visualize the impact on the world, one can imagine the consternation and admiration that would be felt here if the U.S. were to discover suddenly, that some other nation had already put up a successful satellite. . . . In making the decision as to whether or not to undertake construction of such a craft now, it is not inappropriate to view our present situation as similar to that in airplanes prior to the flight of the Wright Brothers. We can see no more clearly now all of the utility and implications of spaceships than the Wright Brothers could see flights of B-29's bombing Japan and air transports circling the globe.[7]

---

[6] Toffler, op. cit., pp. 14, 27. Dr. Olaf Helmer added: "The same statement can probably be made about astronauts, pop singers and Californians." "Science," *Science Journal 3*, no. 10, (October 1967): 49.

[7] "Preliminary Design of an Experimental World-Circling Spaceship," Project RAND Engineering Report to the Army Air Force, Santa Monica, May 1946. Cited in James R. Bright, *Research Development and Technological Innovation* (Homewood, Ill.: Irwin, 1964), p. 9.

Only 11 years later Sputnik electrified the world, and now many high school children, born in the satellite age, regard such flights with bored disdain!

Technological forecasting is nondeterministic, probabilistic assessment (on a relatively high confidence level) of future technology transfer rather than a straight prediction. Such assessments differ from intuition or informal opinion in that "they rest upon an explicit set of quantitative relationships and stated assumptions; and they are produced by a logic that yields relatively consistent results."[8] Hopefully, the various methods replace haphazard stumbling with comprehensive and systematic analyses.

There are over two dozen basic techniques, but the most widely used include the following.

Trend Extrapolation   Growth trends, usually exponential, can be subjected to considerable sophisticated analysis. For example, envelope curves that hypothetically describe the maximum performance available for any particular functional characteristics permit the forecasting of future breakthroughs (be it the energy available from atom smashers, the speed of computers, or the introduction of the electric automobile). Use of such curves may become less accurate as developments over time are influenced by normative thinking or depend on complex interactions.

Morphological Research   This is an exploratory approach that attempts to break up a problem into its basic parameters. For example, a simple chemical jet engine with 11 basic parameters (such as thrust generation, thrust augmentation, energy conversion process, etc.) may be reduced to 25,344 possible simple engines! Some are quite novel—such as the interplanetary aeroduct, the rocket pulse, some hydro engines, and the "terrajet," which may extract minerals from the earth's crust.[9]

---

[8] James R. Bright, ed., *Technological Forecasting for Industry and Government* (Englewood Cliffs, N.J.: Prentice-Hall, 1968), p. xi. This book contains the best concise descriptions of forecasting methods by different proponents. Much has been written on each method; for example, Dr. Robert U. Ayres expanded his discussion on envelope curves in his later book, *Technological Forecasting and Long Range Planning* (New York: McGraw-Hill, 1969).

[9] Erich Jantsch, "Forecasting the Future," *Science Journal 3*, no. 10, October 1967, 40–45. An extensive study of applications in 13 countries is Erich Jantsch, *Technological Forecasting in Perspective* (Paris: O.C.E.D., 1966).

Scenario Writing Perfected at the Hudson Institute, this technique tries to establish a logical sequence of events in order to show how, starting from any given point, a future state might evolve, step by step. The primary purpose is not to predict the future but systematically to explore branching points that are dependent on critical choices.

Normative Relevance Tree Techniques Here the goals are known but the problems must be specified. The branches, or alternatives, are then traced to a number of tips representing deficiencies in the existing state of technology. For example, NASA applied the concept to its Apollo program payload evaluation and discovered some 2300 technological deficiencies to be overcome. Criteria and numerical concepts are introduced at each level of relevance so that "relevance figures" can be calculated for the R&D programs needed: Thus, priorities are established for allocating funds.

Dynamic Models These are models experiencing a change in parameters with time, and their design and application in technological forecasting are in their infancy. Though most are complex and computer based, they are still very dependent on intuition for the basic relationships, the degree of success expected, and the number of expert opinion inputs. Three of the best-known resource allocation models are Profile (a Navy model used to develop a profile of risk, military utility, and technical feasibility); Pattern (developed by Honeywell and based on a relevance tree or an eight-level structured decision network); and Probe I and II, which are modified Delphi exercises (to be discussed) used to produce logic networks or maps of TRW's technological future.[10]

Delphi Technique This is the most widely used and talked about forecasting device, a development of Olaf Helmer of RAND. Delphi is essentially refined brainstorming with the aim of sharpening expert group consensus in a succession of iterative "written rounds"; the carefully chosen experts never meet. In the first round, each responds to the selected topic, such as a forecast of inventions. The replies are analyzed and the most frequent responses returned for a reaction in a second round, in which the experts are to estimate the probability of the listed breakthroughs occurring within a distant future (such

[10] H. W. Lanford, *Technological Forecasting Methodologies* (New York: American Management Association, 1972), pp. 145–152. This is a concise, fairly clear summary for the layman of forecasting techniques and points of view.

as 50 years). The third round would show the median and interquartile estimates (the interval containing the middle 50 percent of the responses) and ask for more exact probabilistic estimates—such as when they will occur with a 10 percent, 50 percent, and 90 percent probability. Experts may change their minds, and those with deviant opinions are asked to justify them. The supporting arguments for extreme positions are distributed in subsequent rounds. The rounds may be repeated several times, with the replies being successively refined without introducing extraneous "face saving" in face-to-face discussion. A famous example of the technique is shown in Exhibit 1.

Currently, hundreds of American corporations use Delphi; they include TRW (a pioneer),[11] McDonnell Douglas, Weyerhaeuser, and Smith, Kline and French. In 1970, TRW reportedly had some 14 panels at work, with 17 experts on each. The Institute of the Future used Delphi to create development options for Connecticut for the next 30 years and to map the future of Du Pont employee fringe benefits.[12] A refinement, called the cross-impact method, uses a matrix to estimate the enhancing or inhibiting influence of one event, occurring as predicted, on another, given an estimated knowledge of diffusion time.

One of the most complete and interesting published examples of the Delphi technique focuses on developments in the life insurance industry up to the year 2000. The text includes all the questionnaires filled out by the 58-member panel together with extensive background material on the industry.[13]

environmental monitoring

In addition to combining social and political trends, corporate strategists are trying to analyze and integrate all the relevant environmental trends. Some have established formal systems for environmental scanning and monitoring. A survey of practice as of the early 1960s was published in Aguilar's *Scanning the*

[11] H. Q. North and Donald L. Pyke, " 'Probes' of the Technological Future," *Harvard Business Review* 47, no. 3 (May–June 1969): 68–76.

[12] "Forecasters Turn to Group Guesswork," *Business Week*, March 14, 1970, p. 134.

[13] Robert I. Mehr and Seev Neumann, *Inflation, Technology, and Growth: Possible Long Range Implications for Insurance* (Bloomington: Indiana University Graduate School of Business, 1972).

exhibit one

AN EXAMPLE OF THE DELPHI TECHNIQUE:
RAND SCIENTISTS PEER INTO THE FUTURE, 1963

	ONE-FOURTH THOUGHT BY THIS DATE	ONE-HALF BY THIS DATE	THREE-FOURTHS BY THIS DATE
Economical desalination of sea water	1964	1970	1980
Ultra-light synthetic construction materials	1970	1971	1978
Automated language translators	1968	1972	1976
New organs through transplanting or prosthesis	1968	1972	1982
Reliable weather forecasts	1972	1975	1988
Wide-access central data storage facility	1971	1979–80	1991
Reformation of physical theory	1975	1980	1993
Implanted plastic or electronic organs	1975	1982	1988
Popular use of personality control drugs	1980	1983	2000
Lasers in X and Gamma ray spectrum region	1978	1985	1989
Controlled thermonuclear power	1980	1986–87	2000
Creation of primitive form of artificial life	1979	1989	2000
Economical ocean-floor mining (other than off-shore drilling)	1980	1989	2000
Limited weather control	1987	1990	2000
Commercial production of synethetic protein for food	1985	1990	2003
Greatly improved physical or chemical therapy for psychotics	1983	1992	2017
General immunization against bacterial and viral diseases	1983	1994	2000
Chemical control over some hereditary defects	1990	2000	2010
Producing 20% of the world's foods by ocean farming	2000	2000	2017
Growth of new organs and limbs through biochemical stimulation	1995	2007	2040
Using drugs to raise intelligence level	1984	2012	2050
Direct electromechanical interaction between man's brain and computer	1990	2020	3000+
Extending life span 50 years by chemical control of aging	1995	2050	2070
Breeding intelligent animals for low-grade labor	2020	2040	3000+
Two-way communication with extra-terrestrials	2000	2075	3000+
Commercial manufacture of chemical elements from subatomic building blocks	2007	2100	3000+
Control of gravity	2035	2050	3000+
Direct information recording on brain	1997	2600	3000+
Long-duration coma for time travel	2006	3000+	3000+
Use of telepathy and ESP in communications	2040	3000+	3000+

SOURCE: *Business Week*, March 14, 1970, p. 130.

Business Environment, and subsequent research studies have illustrated both the process and the information secured in such companies as Coca-Cola or General Electric.[14]

General Electric established a Business Environmental Studies Staff in 1967 to survey and monitor key social, political, and economic trends, and in 1971 undertook long-term environmental forecasting for strategic planning. Nine inputs were selected—geopolitical/defense, international economic, social, political, legal, economic, technological, manpower, and financial.

> In each of these separate "tunnel visions" of specific aspects of the future we tried to (a) give a brief historical review (1960–1970) as a jumping-off point for our analysis of the future; (b) analyze the major future forces for change—a benchmark forecast for 1970–1980; (c) identify the potential discontinuities, i.e., those events which might have low probability, but high significance for General Electric; and (d) raise the first-order questions and policy implications suggested by these forecasts.[15]

Constructing a consistent configuration of the future from such segmented views was done with "cross-impact analysis." The 75 events or trends with the highest probability and importance (to GE) ratings were selected and of each one the question posed: "If this event happens, what will be the effect in the other 74?" The result was sets of domino chains, with one event triggering another. Finally, four scenarios (one most probable and three alternates) were developed. As one forecaster commented: "Significantly, I think, we rated even the benchmark forecast no more than a fifty percent probability. That, at least, is a measure of our own uncertainty about the future."

Many firms support or buy outside research. One of the best known, Stanford Research Institute, has been providing long-range planning and forecasting services (often on a joint sponsorship basis) since 1958; results range from broad industry studies to detailed product appraisals, as specified by the client. Broader participation (and presumably, broader expected re-

---

14 Francis J. Aguilar, *Scanning the Business Environment* (New York: Macmillan, 1967). A summary entitled "Strategic Planning: Some Practical Considerations for Top Management" is in Francis J. Aguilar, Robert A. Howell, and Richard R. Vancil, *Formal Planning Systems—1970* (Boston: Harvard Business School, 1970) (ICH 8-17-141), pp. 169–180. The description of the Coca-Cola approach is on pp. 181–212.

15 Ian H. Wilson, op. cit., pp. 24–25.

sults) is shown by the 100 United States and multinational corporations supporting the Hudson Institute's continuing study "The Corporate Environment, 1975–1985." Other firms helped finance The Institute of the Future, which was established in 1968 with the help of The Conference Board and Olaf Helmer (who left RAND) to study the next 5 to 25 years (or more) and help shape the options to be chosen.

But however well the environmental trends are integrated and monitored, the problem for top management remains: how to bridge the gap between *environmental trends* and specific product or service *opportunities*. Sometimes the gap is filled with some simplifying assumptions and increasingly questionable data extrapolation. More often, as in the TV example cited previously, the gap seems too big and the environmental data are ignored.

The gap has the best chance of being filled through the *complete integration* of technological forecasting and research planning with the rest of the long-range planning process. As one outstanding authority, Erich Jantsch, has demonstrated, such integration requires a completely different approach to planning than the extrapolation of past trends:

> Technological forecasting, like corporate planning, originally developed along the lines of a deterministic approach to planning. It adopted the characteristic principles of linearity and sequentiality, to which the rather indiscriminate use of time-series relating to single technical parameters still bears testimony.
>
> In this primitive form, technological forecasting provided certain inputs to extrapolative planning, but did not interact with other elements of the planning process. It was, in its extreme interpretation, regarded as an objective source of truth about the future, external to planning and human action.
>
> . . .
>
> Technologies are developed to match needs. The deterministic approach to planning inherently assumed that specific technologies correspond to specific needs in an unambiguous way. All that needed to be done for technological forecasting in this framework of sequential problem-solving was to identify needs and technologies and match them. The additional assumption of linearity in extrapolative forecasting tacitly assumed that linear trends of technological parameters or capabilities automatically benefited goals of the future in the same way as they had benefited goals of the past.[16]

[16] Erich Jantsch, *Technological Planning and Social Futures* (New York: Wiley, 1972), pp. 46–47.

Harking back to Galbraith's concern that the inertia of linear technological development will result in setting pseudo-goals,[17] Jantsch makes the case for normative, nondeterministic planning that looks at "possible futures," brings potential future technologies into focus, and delineates goals for scientific and technological planning. Such an approach widens the forecasting time horizon and embraces qualitative goals, including those of desired social missions (such as equal opportunity or minority employment).

Full integration of technological forecasting into corporate planning will come with making "normative" and "explorative" forecasting a completely iterative process. Normative forecasting starts with delineating alternate future goals, while explorative forecasting begins with today's "state of the art" and explores future feasibilities and probabilities. The gap between the two poles is filled only if both goals and feasibilities are regarded as *adaptive inputs* of the *feedback cycle,* not as rigid points to be fitted together. "The search for new and more suitable opportunities goes hand in hand with the adaptation of goals to technological feasibilities and higher probabilities."[18] Fundamental research is stimulated and guided through the "dialogue" between environmental "functional targets" on the one hand and technological "potentialities and limitations" on the other.

STRATEGY IMPLEMENTATION

During the 1960s the conceptual framework for formulating strategy was disseminated and refined. The 1970s face an even more severe challenge: constructing and refining a viable framework for implementing strategy at the top-management level.

Much work remains to be done, but the groundwork was laid a dozen years ago with the publication of the late Douglas M. McGregor's *The Human Side of Enterprise.*[19] As his colleague, Warren G. Bennis, pointed out in a now-famous article, "Revisionist Theory of Leadership," McGregor, "more than other recent students of organizational behavior, has attempted to

[17] John K. Galbraith, *The New Industrial State* (Boston: Houghton Mifflin, 1967).
[18] Erich Jantsch, *Technological Planning and Social Futures,* op. cit., p. 48.
[19] Douglas M. McGregor, *The Human Side of Enterprise* (New York: McGraw-Hill, 1960).

stress the sticky problem of the integration of task requirements with the individual's growth."[20]

The integration is complex and involves linking two completely different—and often antagonistic—theories of management. On the one hand, there is the classical theorist or the scientific management school. Its roots date from about 1910 with Max Weber and Frederick W. Taylor, but the belief in depersonalized work measurements and rational organizational structuring remains and is often voiced, especially in Europe, by such authorities as Lyndall F. Urwick.

To illustrate this approach, Professor Bennis cited Henry Ford as saying, "All we ask of the men is that they do the work which is set before them" and concluded:

> . . . man was viewed as a passive, inert instrument, performing the tasks assigned to him.
>
> In classical theory, then, the conflict between the man and the organization was neatly settled in favor of the organization. The only road to efficiency and productivity was to surrender man's needs to the service of the bloodless machine.[21]

Exaggeration—yes, but Professor Bennis wanted to polarize the viewpoints. In fact, the cost of past mistakes can be seen by (1) designing an ideal organization chart without the incumbent positions or people and (2) comparing it with the actual current version. The ideal chart can provide an objective to be approached with caution but certitude.

The opposing group, the human relations school, thrived from 1930 to 1950. It began with such luminaries as Elton Mayo, Fritz Roethlisberger, W. J. Dickson, and more recently, Carl Rogers. Emphasis was on workers' feelings, attitudes, beliefs, needs, perceptions, ideas, norms, sentiments, and so forth, rather than on the formal structure. As Professor Bennis said, with purposeful exaggeration,

> This model assumes that there is no essential conflict between individual satisfaction and organizational satisfaction, that the former (whether described as "morale," "job satisfaction," or whatever) will lead to greater efficiency, and that authority, insofar as it exists, attempts to facilitate forces which will increase personal satisfaction.[22]

[20] Warren G. Bennis, "Revisionist Theory of Leadership," *Harvard Business Review 31*, no. 1 (January–February 1961): 148.

[21] Ibid., pp. 27–28.

[22] Ibid., pp. 28.

But as the 1950s rolled on, it became increasingly apparent to classical theorists, organizational behavior researchers, and interested businessmen alike that the conflict just described was real and its resolution perhaps the most difficult task faced by a general manager. The dichotomy between personal and business goals was there, even if not so apparent as in the militant late 1960s.

Again McGregor spelled out the challenge:

> The central principle which derives from theory Y is that of integration: the creation of conditions such that members of the organization can achieve their own goals *best* by directing their efforts toward the success of the enterprise.[23]

If the *formulation* of strategy involves looking at the environment on the one hand, looking at present or potential company resources on the other, and effecting some viable integration between the two, then *implementation* of strategy involves integrating the *task* needs of the business and the *personal* needs of employees, thus producing a social climate in which the strategy can be accomplished. Strategy formulation *ends* with plans being split up into meaningful task assignments for divisions, functional areas, departments, and individuals; strategy implementation starts with the same task and tries to relate employee needs to it. Exhibit 2 illustrates the process.

[23] McGregor, op. cit., p. 49.

exhibit two

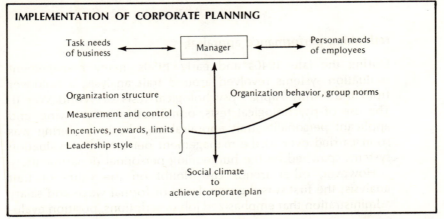

IMPLEMENTATION OF CORPORATE PLANNING

Task needs of business ⟷ Manager ⟷ Personal needs of employees

Organization structure
Measurement and control
Incentives, rewards, limits
Leadership style

Organization behavior, group norms

Social climate
to
achieve corporate plan

linking tasks and needs

Unfortunately, it is much easier to describe the role of strategy implementation than to detail how it should be accomplished; the conceptual framework lacks the specifics and elegance of the formulation counterpart that has been nurtured over some 15 years. Much more research on the role of the general manager—what he does from day to day—is needed before the gaps can be filled properly.

Still, as shown in Exhibit 2, some outlines are clear. The linkage between formal organization and strategy was traced in Chapter 5; the organizational behavior texts are replete with the need to relate the formal organization to the informal. As anyone who ever belonged to any sizable formal organization knows, the lines on the chart may signify intended authority and responsibility relationships, but they in no way indicate actual communication.

Much work has been done over the past 15 years on the subject of variable budgets and other control systems. As pointed out in Chapter 2, well-designed control systems aim to provide the manager with the *information* he needs to do his job better and the *standards* for judging his performance and monitoring the results. Viewed in this perspective—rather than as a means of giving top management a club—the control system does help link personal needs and business tasks, if strictly within the context of job performance.

But it is the evaluation and reward structure that seems to promise the most help during the 1970s in integrating personal and corporate needs. The reasons may be found in the history of performance appraisal since World War II.

rethinking performance appraisal

During the late 1940s and early 1950s, many management evaluation systems revolved around trait analysis, a holdover from the "Army Alpha" psychological tests of World War II. The use of psychological tests, nondirective interviewing, and applicant personality trait appraisal as a basis for hiring was soon carried over to the management performance evaluation systems spawned by the burgeoning personnel departments.

However, other trends cast doubt on the value of trait analysis; the first was the popularity of formal wage and salary administration that emphasized job descriptions, position evaluation, and consistent organization structure. Drawing up a position description for every job in the company and analyzing each as to relative value led many managers to take another look at job content and results. Quantified evaluation methods, such as the point system or factor comparison, raised the question as to whether results shouldn't be quantified also.

The second trend meshed nicely with the first. This was the rise of quantified control systems—especially the concept of return on investment (ROI) and the variable budget. The first became common during the late 1950s, the latter during the early 1960s. Superimposed on formalized wage and salary administration, the new quantitative controls suggested that managers could be judged on a number—be it ROI or meeting the budget. Management accountants may inveigh against such simplistic tools, but many survive today.

The third trend was the use of multiple evaluation criteria or the mixing of quantitative indexes with qualitative traits. A landmark was the 1952 General Electric "measurements project," which proposed eight key result areas (or indexes) for evaluating managers. These areas were

1. Profitability—dollars of residual income (after a capital charge)
2. Market position—percent share
3. Productivity—value added ÷ payroll and depreciation (all adjusted for price level changes)
4. Product leadership
5. Personnel development
   a. Ratio: men promoted/promotable
   b. Percentage ratings: improving, acceptable, deteriorating
6. Employee attitudes
7. Public responsibility
8. Balance between short- and long-range goals.

Clearly, this is quite a mixture of objective and (as in the last three) largely subjective criteria. Still, the project pioneered the idea of using multiple criteria and including objective measurements.

The fourth trend was the increasing explicitness of published corporate objectives and quantification of supporting goals. It was becoming clearer whether the company or division was leading.

Fifth was the rise of formal planning systems, usually unconnected with the stated corporate objectives and strategy. As detailed in Chapter 4, these systems increased the awareness that *everybody plans* in an organization; the need for continuous coordination became paramount. Also, formal planning and budgeting became linked during the late 1960s as more and more firms made the first year of their five-year plan the budget.

the rise of MBO

These five trends combined to foster a new evaluation system —management by objectives, or MBO. The founders were Peter Drucker and Douglas McGregor, but the ideas of evaluating managers on results—the ability to meet previously self-set goals and plans—did not take hold until about 1968. By 1974 there were numerous books on MBO, the majority being "how to do it" cookbooks, and several consulting companies doing a brisk business explaining the concept.[24]

Essentially, MBO is "a method of associating objectives with positions and linking these objectives together and with the corporate plan."[25] The system starts with a manager setting objectives that, within the context of corporate strategy, are quantitative rather than qualitative, specific rather than general, results or *output* oriented rather than activity or *input* centered, realistic and attainable, and with explicit time dimensions. The objectives are approved by the superior to be sure that they are sufficiently challenging, fall within the manager's resources and authority to accomplish, are arranged in order of corporate priorities, are consistently linked with other functional areas both vertically and horizontally, and will have *verifiable, measurable* results. The objectives are then converted into plans of action. At specified intervals (such as every quarter) the results are evaluated by both the manager and his superior and any corrective action agreed upon and implemented. A typical format is shown in Exhibit 3.

MBO has experienced both increasing popularity and some

---

[24] Two of the best overall discussions are George S. Odiorne, *Management by Objectives: A System of Managerial Leadership* (New York: Pitman, 1965), and Harold Koontz, *Appraising Managers as Managers* (New York: McGraw-Hill, 1971). A good "cookbook" version is W. J. Reddin, *Effective Management by Objectives* (New York: McGraw-Hill, 1971).

[25] Reddin, op. cit., p. 12.

common failings. Unfortunately, many American applications of MBO have been undertaken by the personnel area, with the emphasis on management development coupled with a philosophy of "participative management"; the role of corporate strategy is slight indeed. In Europe, especially in the United Kingdom, MBO is properly seen as an integral part of the corporate planning process: The issuance of top management's planning parameters starts the process and provides the necessary coordination focus and boundaries. Also, with personnel development in mind, managers have tended to start MBO at the bottom of the organization rather than the top; often the process never gets beyond front-line management. Again, the quantification of objectives, especially for such staff jobs as training or safety, proves so difficult that the program lapses into a series of qualitative hopes.

However, a rigorous, quantified MBO program can provide the needed framework to make planning a consistent reality throughout the organization. But since MBO looks more at short-run than long-run results, the next challenge is to enlarge the perspective and devise new methods of management compensation. General Electric is doing this with the SBU managers, but viable solutions are yet to be proved.

leadership style

The most important ingredient for strategy implementation is the leadership skills of the general manager. Research on the general manager at work indicates that successful chief executives develop a style of leadership that includes the following skills:

1. *Seeing everything in a multidimensional perspective.* The general manager should see the smallest task, for example, both as a necessary detail in the mosaic of corporate strategy and as the whole mission of some one person.
2. *Being sensitive to reality.* The general manager should know (a) what is actually going on in the environment and (b) the personal needs of others in order to be aware of *what* changes are acceptable and *when* they will be understood in terms of group norms.
3. *Setting timed priorities.* The general manager should be aware of which decisions are so important, given the stage of the organization's development or the state of the in-

exhibit three

EXAMPLE OF MBO GOAL SETTING AND EVALUATION

Participant: Frank E. Burke, Sales Mgr.   Division: Building Products
Verifiable Goal No.: 1   Target Date for
                                                                     Accomplishment

BRIEF STATEMENT:

Establish Do-It-Yourself Market

A. Develop package designed to be marketed through
   cooperating hardware manufacturers, to be made
   available to their distributors under a private label.   April 1

B. Develop complete program, including merchandising
   rack, to promote do-it-yourself products.   July 1

Results expected: Sales on this program will total
$300,000 with a gross profit of $105,000.   December 31

FIRST-QUARTER REVIEW:

The package has been developed. It will be made available to cooperating
manufacturers in June and to our distributors in August. We now expect sales
of $225,000 with a gross margin of 45 percent giving us a gross profit of
$68,250.

Superior's comments:

SECOND-QUARTER REVIEW:

The package, in a rough stage, was shown to three manufacturers in June. They
expressed great interest, and the assistant sales manager will have a complete
package with him on a trip to manufacturers in late August or early September.
The complete package with merchandise rack will be introduced to the district

dustry, that he must make them, and which ones he can
afford to let others make.

4. *Producing a system of limits.* A general manager should
   seek agreement on the framework of objectives, policies,
   plans, tasks, and so on that can produce a system of
   limits within which people are free to act on their own.

5. *Infusing shared values.* The general manager can use
   symbols (such as a new corporate logo or headquarters
   decor) to signify change and institutionalize values.

6. *Creating an atmosphere.* Mostly through example and
   practice, a general manager can create a consistent personal philosophy of management—an atmosphere in which

sales managers at the sales meeting in October and immediately afterwards to the distributors. Sales are now expected to reach $180,000 with a gross profit of $51,000.

Superior's comments: Essentially, dates have been met (parts A and B). Sales (results) must await December 31 for evaluation.—LEJ

THIRD-QUARTER REVIEW:

The complete package was introduced to the DSMs at the sales meeting. It appears that because of deliveries on the part of the vendors, we will not be in a position to introduce this product to distributors until the middle of December. After considering the value of a mid-December introduction, I am going to hold this product line until the January market to get the full impact. The result is that we will have no sales in this year and I will not have reached my objective.

Superior's comments: Agree—goal not accomplished.—LEJ

FOURTH-QUARTER REVIEW:

As outlined in the Third-Quarter Review, we withheld the introduction of this product line until the January market. As a result, there were no sales for 1969. Initial results from market introduction indicate that we will exceed our forecasts and could total as much as $800,000 for 1970.

Superior's comments: This project, although behind Frank's schedule, was launched in excellent fashion and promises results well in excess of his forecast in 1970.—LEJ

SOURCE: Adapted from Harold Koontz, *Appraising Managers as Managers* (New York: McGraw-Hill, 1971), pp. 200–202.

people can identify with organizational goals and values and find fulfillment.

Clearly, this list is unfinished. Much expensive, time-consuming, difficult-to-release research still remains to be done on the general manager; however, the essence of the job of implementing strategy and providing leadership was effectively summarized over 20 years ago:

In a very broad and much more real sense than is generally supposed, the administrative leader is trying to integrate the needs of the organization with the requirements of the individual for growth and personal development. Unless he understands people as individuals and realizes their expectations, as well as those of the group as a whole, he will not have defined the limits or the opportunities of his work. . . . The concept of the leader as one who helps the organization to do is in fact vastly broader in scope than the concept of the leader as one who holds the helm alone.[26]

[26] Edmund P. Learned, David N. Ulrich, and Donald R. Booz, *Executive Action* (Boston: Division of Research, Harvard Business School, 1951), pp. 208, 211.

seven

CONCLUSION

An understanding of business policy gleaned from the preceding pages is interesting, but soon forgotten if not applied. The next step for the practicing manager is to dust off the company (or divisional or functional area) strategy and planning statements to see if they are still relevant. A checklist to help in this appraisal is included in Appendix B.

Some managers will have to start from scratch and write strategies and plans; often these will be functional area plans on either the corporate or the divisional level. The approach will be the same for any size of company, level, or function. For example, The Conference Board has compiled a most useful selection of procedures for marketing planning,[1] while Frank Gilmore details how a small company should plan and make certain the feedback loop is closed.[2]

Students and managers alike will want to browse further in the field in addition to pursuing particular areas of interest through footnoted sources. Everyone should start with Peter Drucker's *The Practice of Management*,[3] which solidified so much of the conceptual foundation for the strategy and planning process, and *Concept of the Corporation*,[4] a fascinating study of General Motors in the 1940s, reissued in 1972 with a critical postscript.

Three books in particular provide a picture of industry thought and practice. In *Long-Range Planning in American Industry*,[5] Brian W. Scott discusses the current state of the art as

[1] David S. Hopkins, *The Short-Term Marketing Plan* (New York: The Conference Board, 1972).

[2] Frank F. Gilmore, "Formulating Strategy in Smaller Companies," *Harvard Business Review 49*, no. 3 (May–June 1971): 71–81.

[3] Peter F. Drucker, *The Practice of Management* (New York: Harper & Row, 1954).

[4] Peter F. Drucker, *Concept of the Corporation*, rev. ed. (New York: Day, 1972).

[5] Brian W. Scott, *Long Range Planning in American Industry* (New York: American Management Association, 1965).

of 1965 with numerous examples and some historical perspective. Nor should one miss George A. Steiner's mammoth tome, *Top Management Planning*,[6] which combines extensive library research with a pragmatic conceptual framework. The second half of the book focuses mainly on various planning tools such as linear programing and the product life cycle; the bibliography too is worthwhile. Further examples of formal planning, plus a good selection of readings, are contained in the third edition of David Ewing's *Long Range Planning for Management*.[7]

Those wishing to pursue the conceptual aspects of the field will enjoy Kenneth Andrews' *The Concept of Corporate Strategy*.[8] Aside from some semantic differences, the framework is similar to the one proposed here; both had their origins at the Harvard Business School.

Because strategy and planning is a rapidly evolving field, one is faced with the problem of keeping up. Probably more articles pertaining to strategy appear in the *Harvard Business Review* than in any other major publication.[9] However, it is even better to pose strategy questions to oneself—What is the *key skill* needed here? What *strategy alternatives* are available? —when reading any business story, be it in the *Wall Street Journal, Business Week,* or even the local paper. Thinking in a strategic way is a prime requisite to acting.

Of course, the best way to keep up with strategy and planning is to practice it, to approach every situation, problem, proposal, or decision with a general management point of view. By doing this one develops the ability to spot and size up any situation in terms of the short- and long-run implications for the *whole* company.

[6] George A. Steiner, *Top Management Planning* (London: Macmillan, 1969).

[7] David W. Ewing, ed., *Long Range Planning for Management,* 3d ed. (New York: Harper & Row, 1972).

[8] Kenneth R. Andrews, *The Concept of Corporate Strategy* (Homewood, Ill.: Dow Jones–Irwin, 1971).

[9] Supplementary readings in the field of business policy should include such collections as Robert J. Mockler, ed., *Readings in Business Planning and Policy Formulation* (New York: Appleton, 1972).

appendix A

THE ART OF CASE PREPARATION

How often have you heard that "you only learn by experience"? The inclusion of cases in business policy courses is based on this belief, so widely shared by practicing managers. Discussing business cases permits a pooling of the broad, cumulative experience and collective wisdom found among the participants; the case merely provides a common focus. It is the responsibility of the class to produce a lively, interesting, and intellectually challenging discussion.

Clearly, the instructor plays an unusual role. He is not a lecturer or an expounder of principles lifted from the textbook; rather, he serves as a catalyst or coach. He may be a helpful source of information, but more often he asks probing questions and has the irritating ability to put his finger on just those areas that the participant has not fully thought out.

At the end of the class, the instructor may make a few summary comments, or he may simply walk away to the clamor of, "But what's the right answer?" "What did the company do?" "What would you do?" To him, all three questions are irrelevant. What is relevant is what each person in the class thinks *he* would do after having identified the problems in the situation, pinpointed all the available data, made explicit any necessary assumptions, analyzed each problem in depth, and examined the possible alternative solutions and their implications. In short, each person must make a decision and, in so doing, see the alternate decisions he might have made and fully evaluate why he didn't choose those courses. Furthermore, he must understand why others don't agree with his decision.

There are no right answers to a business case, because (1) each situation is unique and (2) there is no one "right" way to run a company. Rather, the case asks each participant, What does this unique situation *demand* that *you* do or have done? Each manager has to develop a style that is suited not only to himself but also to the type of industry, company, and environment in which he finds himself. Two managers faced with the same situation may make diametrically opposed decisions, each equally workable. With a business case one comes face-to-face with the fact that there is no comfortable solution.

Discussing cases therefore can be very frustrating. The more the participant gets involved in the discussions and commits himself to a certain line of action by vigorous participation, the more he will be frustrated by the inability of others to see the correctness of his viewpoint. He will be frustrated by finding that he forgot a whole range of problems, facts, or solutions when studying the case by himself.

Very careful preparation is essential for a good case discussion. The more thorough the advance preparation, the more stimulating and meaningful the case discussion itself. One method is to read the case quickly to get a general idea of the ground to be covered and then go over it more carefully, always referring to the exhibits *when they are mentioned in the text*. The impact of a particular exhibit may be obscured if the study of exhibits is deferred until later. It is often useful to take notes on the problems or facts that seem relevant to the analysis you have done, or to the alternate conclusions that seem possible. Be sure to explore as many alternatives as possible rather than adopting the first approach that seems reasonable.

Discussing the case in a small group before class is another must. Such a study group ensures that more than one or two alternatives are explored, facilitates probing the proposed analysis for faulty logic or problems in implementation, and permits dividing up the needed quantitative analysis among the participants. For those who are "lost" on a particular case—and everyone flounders once in a while—the study group is a source of help and advice. And those who are a bit hesitant about expressing their views before a large group are often the most active participants in preclass study sessions.

"But the case doesn't have enough facts, we need more information," some study group member is sure to say with dismay. Unfortunately, the same lament can be made about most of the data on which management decisions are made. A manager frequently must make far-reaching decisions on seemingly inadequate information in the face of considerable uncertainty. A case forces the participant to go through the very realistic process of making sure all relevant information is used and, if more is needed, specifying exactly what is needed and how the supplying of the missing data will affect the decision. Sometimes such analysis shows that actually the "needed" information, if available, would not change the decision. Many experienced executives claim that cases tend to be unrealistic in providing too much, not too little, information; they are accustomed to basing decisions on less.

Quantifying case decisions helps ensure that all the information has been used, facilitates communication among the participants, and fosters an in-depth discussion of specifics rather than a glossing over of generalities. Considerable time may be saved if as much analysis as possible is done before getting out a slide rule. In other words, discover where quantitative analysis would help first, rather than "pushing every number in sight." On the other hand, once the areas for "number pushing" have been identified, the participant should beware of giving up too easily. He should make assumptions as needed and see how far creative, imaginative quantification can go.

Class participation is both fun and a significant learning experience. It is a chance to put one's ideas out in public and hear them criticized constructively and become part of a consensus. Sometimes it is difficult to realize when your pet ideas are attacked that it is not you as a person being attacked, but only your point of view on the particular case. Of course, just because your ideas are attacked doesn't mean they are wrong; they may be very suitable for you but not necessarily for others. It is even harder to listen carefully to other people's divergent point of view, compare them with yours, and perhaps change your mind.

Students of business policy often ask whether the cases are real. Almost invariably, the case is a faithful picture of a particular business situation as seen and recorded by the case writer. Much effort is expended to ensure that the "slice of life" pictured is representative. Most cases are collected by researchers who approach a company on the basis of an article in the press, a suggestion by one of the managers, or a tip from a friend, former student, or associate. The case writer spends several days in the field recording data and then attempts to reproduce what he found in the space of a few mimeographed pages. Before using any of the results, he must obtain written releases from the company. Sometimes company executives visit the classes to hear the unbiased reactions of participants.

In the end, however, one learns about the case method by experiencing it, not by reading. It is time to forget one's normal occupation and substitute a vicarious experience. "Now, if you were that executive, what *exactly* would you do?"

appendix B

CHECKLIST FOR CORPORATE OR DIVISIONAL STRATEGY

I. The corporate image or divisional charter
   A. Does it clearly answer the questions
      1. What business are we in?
         a. Market—customers and customer needs
         b. Product—divisional area
      2. What kind of company or division are we or do we want to become?
         a. Broadens horizons
         b. Sets boundaries—"a system of limits"—or focus
   B. Is it realistic in view of
      1. Changing internal skills?
      2. Changing environmental trends?
II. Corporate or divisional objectives
   A. Do they clearly answer the question
      1. Where is the company or division going, and when is it going to get there?
         a. Quantified, measurable output content
         b. Related to company or group objectives
         c. Short- and long-run objectives (goals) consistent
         d. Priorities clear and agreed upon
   B. Do they reflect management's goals, values, aspirations?
      1. Acceptable level of risk
      2. Sociopolitical values
   C. Are they based on a realistic assessment of past performance?
      1. Market audit
         a. Market segmentation
         b. Product mix
         c. Market forecast
         d. Price forecast
         e. Purchasing patterns

2. Competition audit
   a. Competitive climate
   b. Capacity utilization
   c. Competitive assets (design, product, finance, market, performance, etc.)
   d. Price, volume mix analysis
D. Do they reflect strengths and weaknesses?
   1. Relative to competition
   2. Quantified
      a. Relevant costs and contribution
      b. Break-even analysis
      c. Price sensitivity
      d. Profit sensitivity
E. Are they built on our distinctive competence (unique skills)?
   1. Human
   2. Physical assets
   3. Financial
   4. Intangible (such as goodwill)
F. Are they aimed at attainable opportunities?
   1. Broad trends
      a. Social
      b. Political
      c. Economic
         (1) Markets
         (2) Customers
         (3) Industry
         (4) Suppliers
      d. Technological—evolving forecasting techniques
   2. Assumptions agreed upon
      a. Confidence level specified and quantified
      b. Controllable separated from uncontrollable
G. Are the objectives constantly reevaluated and sensitive indicators pinpointed?
III. Corporate or divisional policies
   A. Do they clearly answer the question
      1. How is the division going to reach its objectives?
         a. Need for consistency
         b. Hierarchy—policies for one level are objectives for another
   B. Are they sufficiently explicit to guide day-to-day decisions?

IV. Corporate or divisional strategic plans
  A. Do they answer the question
    1. What has to be done in all functional areas to reach the objectives?
  B. Do they clearly allocate scarce resources?
    1. Supported by strategic action programs
    2. Consistent with functional area strategies
  C. Do they minimize competitors' advantages?
  D. Are they geared to reality, not management hopes?
    1. Realistic time span to cover all payout periods
    2. Consistent vertically and horizontally throughout the organization (explicit parameters for planning at lower echelons)
  E. Have viable strategy alternatives been formulated and criteria for chosing mix agreed upon?
  F. Has contingency planning been done?
    1. "What if" analysis of assumptions made, including costs if strategy goes wrong
    2. Trigger points specified
  G. Related to strategic action programs?
    1. Strategic expenditure programs (facilities investment schedules)
    2. The variable budget or profit plan (planning versus budgeting)
V. Corporate or divisional feedback system
  A. Does it answer the questions
    1. What do I need to know to plan and do my job better?
      a. Information flows
    2. How am I doing?
      a. Network of standards—a system of limits
  B. Do the budgetary controls really reflect plans, not number juggling?
    1. Pinpointing changes in managed (semifixed) costs as budgeted volume fluctuates
VI. The general management viewpoint
  A. Key skill: seeing the *key* long- and short-term implications for the total enterprise of *any* situation, problem, proposal, or decision
    1. Conceptual versus technical skills
    2. Adequate compromises versus functional optimization

      3. Visionary imagination versus action orientation
B. The ability to spot and size up the essence of any strategic situation

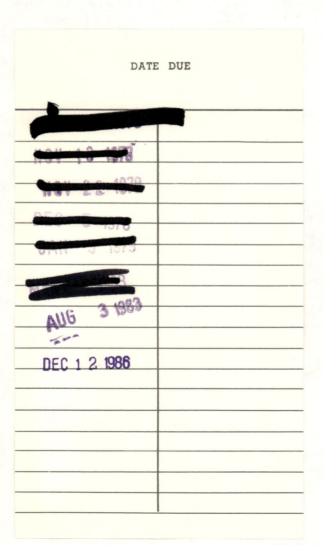

DATE DUE

AUG   3 1983

DEC 1 2 1986